EMPATHIC ATTUNEMENT

THE "TECHNIQUE" OF PSYCHOANALYTIC SELF PSYCHOLOGY

CRAYTON E. ROWE, JR., M.S.W.
DAVID S. MAC ISAAC, Ph.D.

A JASON ARONSON BOOK

ROWMAN & LITTLEFIELD PUBLISHERS, INC.
Lanham • Boulder • New York • Toronto • Oxford

THE MASTER WORK SERIES

A JASON ARONSON BOOK

ROWMAN & LITTLEFIELD PUBLISHERS, INC.

Published in the United States of America
by Rowman & Littlefield Publishers, Inc.
A wholly owned subsidiary of The Rowman & Littlefield Publishing Group, Inc.
4501 Forbes Boulevard, Suite 200, Lanham, Maryland 20706
www.rowmanlittlefield.com

PO Box 317
Oxford
OX2 9RU, UK

British Library Cataloguing in Publication Information Available

Library of Congress Cataloging-in-Publication Data

Rowe, Crayton E.
    Empathic attunement.

    Bibliography: p.
    Includes index.
    1. Self psychology. 2. Psychotherapist and patient. I. Mac Isaac, David S. II. Title.
RC489.S43R68   1989   155.2   88-8069

95-46035

ISBN: 978-0-87668-551-8

Printed in the United States of America

To our children
Clara, Andrew, Sean,
and
David James

Contents

ACKNOWLEDGMENTS

There are many to whom we would like to express thanks for their support and inspiration in the writing of this book. First, of course, we would like to acknowledge Heinz Kohut for his lasting legacy that includes not only his writings but also the courage and integrity he showed in putting forth ideas that were often not popularly received. His contributions are a notable basis for further study, and his example is a model for future psychoanalysts in the presentation of their own innovative and creative ideas.

We also acknowledge the valuable contributions

provided in workshops, conferences, and personal communications by a number of Kohut's intimate collaborators. Among those we would especially like to thank are Paul Ornstein, Anna Ornstein, Arnold Goldberg, and Michael Franz Basch.

We would like to express our gratitude to the members of The Society for the Study of Heinz Kohut's Works, a group formed in 1985. Among those members we would particularly like to thank are Florence Rowe and Joseph Walsh for their important input in our many open and frank exchanges over the years.

We also thank Dr. Jason Aronson for the confidence he showed in our work and the enthusiasm with which he greeted our manuscript. His encouragement and suggestions were invaluable. As well, we want to express our deeply felt appreciation to Dorothy Erstling and Adelle Krauser for their many thoughtful and perceptive comments and questions, which were essential to our book's final form.

We thank the many individuals of the Foxy Copy Center for their helpful suggestions and their cooperative assistance in the typing process that allowed us to put together the manuscript for this book in a timely and orderly manner.

Finally, it goes without saying that this book could never have been completed without the patience and loving support of our families, who were so understanding of the long hours that we had to spend apart from them in order to put this text into its final form.

Crayton E. Rowe, Jr., M.S.W.
New York, New York

David S. Mac Isaac, Ph.D.
Englewood, New Jersey

INTRODUCTION

Perhaps no one since Freud has jogged the collective sensibility of the psychoanalytic community more than Heinz Kohut. Since his celebrated works were introduced, there has been an outpouring of scholarly literature explaining and elaborating on his theories of self psychology, applying them to the existing body of knowledge in the mental health field. Much of this literature, however, including Kohut's own writings, requires psychoanalytic background and training in order to grasp the fundamentals of self psychology. It is clearly time for a clinical text that captures the essence of Kohut's works and presents it in a straightforward, accurate, and usable way. This book was written to meet that need. It introduces Kohut to the student, and at the same time it offers the experienced clinician a synthesis of Kohut's major concepts. In particular, this book highlights Kohut's fundamental contribution, his emphasis on the empathic mode of data gathering from within the patient's experience. Empathic attunement to what the patient is experiencing is a complex human process that involves a high degree of technical skill when applied to the therapeutic clinical situation.

We have presented our clinical material in moment-to-moment detail in an effort to offer a "hands-on" experience for the reader. In this way the reader can participate alongside the analyst as the session unfolds. Of course, we recognize that understanding self psychology, and especially its clinical application, cannot occur simply through the study of theory and case material. The process of becoming a psychoanalytic self psychologist, with its emphasis on the empathic stance, is a complex one. Yet we believe that our method of presentation has important heuristic value for anyone wishing to grasp the full implications of Heinz Kohut's contributions.

To simplify terminology, we have used the word "analyst" as a generic title to identify the psychoanalytic practitioner. This should emphasize the fact that all clinicians may be enriched by the study of self psychology regardless of their level of training.

The vignettes presented to exemplify the theory in Part I and Part II were taken primarily from treatment cases in our own practices. However, some examples were taken from cases presented to us by our supervisees. In all examples, identifying data were disguised to preserve confidentiality. In addition, independent readers were used to further disguise the material while maintaining its essential meaning.

In Part III, Ms. O. and Mr. V. were treated by Crayton

Rowe, Jr., and were similarly disguised to preserve confidentiality and anonymity.

Finally, we believe this book serves as a guide for interested readers outside the mental health field. Kohut's contributions to empathy and to understanding the inner experiences of others are valuable to many audiences – educators, parents, social scientists, and all those whose work demands a deep sensitivity to their fellow human beings.

I

Understanding from the Vantage Point of the Patient's Experience

CHAPTER 1

Kohut the Man

Every scientific theory is the natural outgrowth and extension of its creator, and self psychology is no exception. Although Kohut emphasized that the personality of the author of a scientific work should not influence one's evaluation of the work itself (1984), we think that some appreciation of Kohut's life and how he arrived at his theories will enhance the reader's understanding.

Kohut's theory of the self is both the culmination of his lifelong work and the fullest expression of his unique creativity, empathy, and courage. It is the task of this chapter to offer a brief but personal glimpse at the story of

his life in order to highlight the nodal points at which his unique
gifts led him to his formulations of the theory of the self.

Heinz Kohut was born in Vienna in 1913 and died in 1981
in Chicago, where he had lived for over forty years. There has
been relatively little written about his life, except for a brief
biographical sketch, "Glimpses of a Life: Heinz Kohut," written
by Charles Strozier (1985). Other information about him can be
gleaned from a thumbnail sketch of Kohut's work in *Time* magazine (December 1, 1980), and the obituaries written by Montgomery (1981) and Goldberg (1982).

As an only child, his precocious abilities were recognized at
an early age. He was born in Vienna and spent his childhood and
early adulthood there. He attended the local elementary school
and later the Doblinger Gymnasium where he excelled academ-
ically, and regularly participated in sports such as track and
boxing. His many references to such well-known figures as
Beethoven, Thomas Mann, Dostoyevsky, Horace and the like
derived from his thorough grounding in a classical education that
included Latin, Greek, French, science, and world literature.

Kohut was tutored between the ages of 8 and 14 by a young
university student. This young man played an important role in
his intellectual and emotional development. Goldberg recounts a
"complex and erudite" game that Kohut and his tutor would
play, a version of "Guess What I'm Thinking" and "Twenty
Questions." The objective of the game was to imagine what
would have occurred in world history if a particular event had
not taken place or a particular historical figure had not lived. For
example, how would the world be different if Hannibal had not
crossed the Alps or Caesar had not been assassinated?

This rigorous mental game not only expanded his knowledge of history – something Kohut was noted for – but also developed observational skills similar to those that would serve him so
effectively as a psychoanalyst. Such skills would evolve from the

need to imagine, during this childhood exercise, what it would be like for an individual to live in a certain society or culture.

He went on to study medicine at the University of Vienna and received his medical degree there. During this time he became interested in psychoanalytic ideas and underwent an analysis with August Aichorn. In all his years in Vienna, Kohut never spoke with Freud. However, he frequently recounted having seen his "admired master" at the railroad station when Freud left Vienna to escape the Nazis in 1938. For Strozier the fondness with which Kohut told of this experience suggested ". . . continuities and Viennese connections . . . [and] a special sense of mission that he felt about psychoanalysis as a young man" (p. 6).

Kohut departed from Vienna a few months later. He settled in England for a time and then emigrated to America in 1940. He took his specialty training in neurology at the University of Chicago and was rapidly recognized as one who would have an impact on his field. However, he soon shifted interests and professional pursuits from neurology to psychoanalysis. He received his analytic training at the Chicago Institute for Psychoanalysis, and upon graduation was appointed faculty member and training analyst. This was indeed an honor for one so relatively inexperienced.

He was trained in the classical tradition of psychoanalysis, modified by the clinical and theoretical advances of the American ego psychology school of Hartmann, Kris, and Loewenstein. This tradition was grounded in the two basic Freudian principles of (1) transference: a displacement upon the analyst by the analysand of unconscious incestuous longings that play out the unresolved oedipal drama of childhood and (2) resistance: the unconscious process impeding the recognition of these desires.

Kohut became an advocate of these theories in his teaching, lecturing, and writing, and soon developed the reputation of-being a conservative Freudian theorist. His views brought him the public admiration of such psychoanalytic luminaries as Anna Freud, Kurt Eissler, and Heinz Hartmann. In 1964 he was elected President of the American Psychoanalytic Association. Following this he was elected Vice President of the International Psychoanalytic Association and retained the position for nine years. This period earned him among his colleagues the affectionate title of "Mr. Psychoanalysis."

It was, therefore, surprising when Kohut shifted his clinical views. Many of his colleagues, who had given him so much recognition just a short time before, now rejected him. His writings of the mid to late sixties questioned many of the psychoanalytic principles he had previously defended. But what had occurred to turn him around? What made him question the previously unquestioned? What made him reconsider the very theories of psychoanalysis that had so long guided his thinking and his clinical practice?

Kohut's clinical and theoretical perspective was considerably broadened by the case of Miss F. (Kohut 1968, 1971), which opened his eyes to significantly different psychic perceptions. Briefly, Miss F., a 25-year-old woman, had insisted that Kohut be nearly perfectly attuned to what she was saying. If, for example, he made any intervention that went beyond what she had said or learned in the therapy, she would become enraged. Kohut was initially firm in his theoretical belief that her protests were defensive and hid the underlying issues. Miss F. persisted in her complaints that he was "not listening," that he was "undermining her," that his remarks "had destroyed everything she had built up," and that he was "wrecking her analysis." Kohut realized that she would become calm only when he summarized or repeated what she had already said. Miss F.'s persistence in her complaints, together with Kohut's awareness of what calmed her, helped him to suspend his theoretical assumption that she was being defensive and to understand the importance of her need for confirming and mirroring responses. Furthermore, he realized that his interventions had not only not been helpful but, in fact, were adding to her problems. Through his work with Miss F., Kohut began to formulate his ideas about the developmental need for mirroring, as well as the mirroring selfobject transference.

It was treatment experiences such as these that prompted Kohut, in a letter dated May 16, 1974 (*The Search for the Self,* Vol. 2), to respond so frankly to a fellow scientist, openly admitting that the one factor which had caused him to reconsider his theoretical perspective was the fact that he felt "stumped" by a large percentage of his cases in which treatment either stalemated or was prematurely terminated. In the letter he wrote:

> If I tried to explain their relationship to me, their demands on me, as revivals of their old love and hate for their parents, or for their brothers and sisters, I had more and more the feeling that my explanations became forced and that my patients' complaints that I did not understand them . . . were justified. [pp. 888–889]

His prolonged empathic immersion into the inner worlds of these same patients opened him to new and previously unrecognized psychic configurations. He continued:

> It was on the basis of feeling stumped that I began to entertain the thought that these people were not concerned with me as a separate person but that they were concerned with themselves; that they did not love or hate me, but that they needed me as part of themselves, needed me as a set of functions which they had not acquired in early life; that what appeared to be their love and hate was in reality their need that I fulfill certain psychological functions for them and anger at me when I did not do so. [pp. 888–889]

He outlined his thoughts on narcissism in his paper, "Forms and Transformations on Narcissism," which was published in the Journal of the American Psychoanalytic Association in 1966. This paper formed the nucleus of his first book, *The Analysis of the Self*, published in 1971.

As his ideas began to spread in the late sixties, the rejection of him by his friends and colleagues intensified. Naturally these rejections hurt Kohut deeply, but they did not deter him from continuing his work. Many wanted to brand him as a dissident and to accuse him of founding a new school. However, he remained steadfast in his belief that his theory of the self was a further development and extension of psychoanalysis.

Though he lost a number of his valued friends and supporters, not all of them turned away. Many younger colleagues, who were former students of his and candidates at the Chicago Institute, gathered around him to form a study group similar to Freud's Wednesday Evening Society. They met regularly to discuss his evolving ideas. The initial membership of the group consisted of John Gedo, Arnold Goldberg, Michael Franz Basch, David Marcus, Paul Tolpin, Marian Tolpin, Paul Ornstein, Anna Ornstein, and Ernest Wolf. Over the years many others joined. A valuable purpose of the group was to offer Kohut a buffer against the potentially distracting public attacks of critics and to support him in the completion of his work. The group brought with them an enthusiasm for his ideas that buoyed Kohut and eventually culminated in his 1971 monograph, *The Analysis of the Self*, followed by his 1977 book, *The Restoration of the Self*. *The Psychology of the Self: A Casebook* (Goldberg 1978), exemplifying the theory of self psychology, was another publication generated by this group.

While many of the psychoanalytic community viewed his theory of the self as heretical, there were many who respected his ideas and applied them in their work. Evidence of the growing impact that his theories were having was seen in the high attendance at the annual conferences on self psychology that were held around the country. For example, in 1980, 1,100 mental health professionals attended the Boston conference. As a result of failing health, Kohut felt an urgency to complete his work and was forced to conserve his energy by limiting his speaking engagements. In those instances when he chose not accept an invitation, he frequently sent his trusted colleagues to discuss his ideas and to answer his critics. Unfortunately, this was seen as being "isolationist." It was also interpreted by others as an expression of Kohut's avoidance of facing his critics.

Kohut's final speech, "Reflections on Empathy," was given at the 1981 self psychology conference in Berkeley, California. He was aware that he was dying, and at the conclusion of his speech he announced his final farewell. The audience, moved by his words, stood to express its deep appreciation. When the applause went on and on, Kohut gently raised his hands, interrupting the ovation, and quietly said, "I know your feelings. . . . I want to rest now." He died four days later on Thursday, October 8, 1981.

How Does Analysis Cure? was his final book, published posthumously in 1984. This work offered new perspectives on the place of empathy in analytic cure, and it expanded the concepts of defense and resistance; moreover, perhaps most importantly, it offered directions that we can pursue to understand more fully the human condition.

CHAPTER 2

Empathy – Its Definition and Functions

In his 1959 essay, "Introspection, Empathy, and Psycho-analysis: An Examination of the Relationship Between Mode of Observation and Theory," Kohut speaks of empathy as the major tool of psychoanalysis. By this he simply meant that we can observe thoughts, wishes, feelings, and fantasies only through introspection in our-selves and through vicarious introspection (empathy) in others. He later stated: "The best definition of empathy . . . is that it is the capacity to think and feel oneself into the inner life of another person" (1984, p. 82). From the time of his 1959 paper to his posthumously published

15

monograph, *How Does Analysis Cure?*, he consistently emphasized that only through empathy could one come to an in-depth
understanding of the inner life of another person. In other words,
he believed that it is only through immersion in the patient's
experience that the analyst can hope to gather relevant, in-depth
psychological data as a true basis for clinical understanding and
theory building.

Kohut was not trying to introduce a new formulation of
empathy into the framework of psychoanalysis; rather, he was
attempting to return it to its original place of prominence. He was
deeply concerned that the field of psychology was moving away
from the purely psychological, "experience-near," introspective
mode of data gathering (that had allowed Freud such momentous
discoveries as transference and resistance) to an "experience-
distant," extrospective mode of observation more appropriate to
other sciences such as biology, physics, and sociology. Of course,
Kohut recognized the importance of taking cues from these other
sciences and cross-referencing their findings with those of psychoanalysis, but he believed that the final substantiation for
clinical interpretations and psychoanalytic theories must be
based upon introspection and empathy.

EMPATHY: A HUMAN PROCESS

But how do we go about sensing the inner life of another person?
Perhaps the familiar phrase, "to put oneself into the shoes of
another," best describes this process and most accurately captures
what Kohut means by "experience-near." Simply stated, the
analyst attempts to experience as closely as possible what the
patient is experiencing (an approximation). The nuances of this
process in the clinical setting are discussed in detail later in this

book. But for now, let us consider this normal human process as it occurs regularly among people.

Each of us has an ongoing, continuous flow of inner experiences. These may include our experience of a certain event or situation, such as a rainy day or a difficult task. They may include our experience of another person's experiencing an event or situation. Our experiences also include our own experience of ourselves. And finally, they may also include our experience of others experiencing us as we experience them. This intersubjective process is one that occurs whenever human beings interact.

Let us use a simple example. Your female friend purchases a new car with all the extras such as air-conditioning, stereo sound system, sun roof, and power windows. She is particularly thrilled with herself and her purchase because she has shopped around and feels she has gotten the best buy. She is excited to show you. In turn, you have a series of impressions that are taken in with your senses and that include a total experience of the car itself and of your friend's experience of her new car. You see the glistening new paint and hear the quiet hum of the engine. You feel the plush upholstery and smell the scent of fresh leather. At the same time, you experience your friend's pride in her new purchase and her boastfulness as she describes how she was able to get a good buy. In turn, your friend may experience your being less excited than she is about her purchase. She, in turn, begins to feel some disappointment.

Though this intersubjective flow of experiences may sound complicated in its description, it is a process that goes on in every human interaction. Unless one is a trained clinician, it is not something we think about consciously because our minds have the capacity to perceive and synthesize without our conscious awareness.

Returning to the clinical setting, the analyst's own focus remains consistently upon what the patient is experiencing. This encompasses not only the moment-to-moment experiences of the patient but also the continuous flow of these experiences over time. Kohut refers to the attunement to this continuous flow of moment-to-moment experiences as *prolonged immersion* or as long-term *empathic immersion* in the psychological field (Kohut 1977). **Empathic immersion into the patient's experience focuses the analyst's attention upon what it is like to be the subject rather than the target of the patient's wishes and demands** (Schwaber 1979). The following brief vignettes exemplify this important distinction.

Mr. S., a middle-aged man with a history of work problems, rushed into the consulting room after tossing his rain-soaked coat upon one of the analyst's newly upholstered office chairs. The analyst was concerned about his chair and annoyed by his patient's apparent lack of consideration. Initially viewing himself as the target of the patient's unconscious projections, the analyst interpreted the act as an expression of displaced anger. Mr. S., in turn, became apologetic and immediately removed his coat from the chair.

Realizing in that moment that he had responded to the patient's behavior (outside the patient's experience), the analyst shifted his attention to what Mr. S. was experiencing and away from himself as a target. From this "experience-near" vantage point, he recognized that his patient felt misunderstood and hurt by the interpretation. The analyst communicated this understanding and, furthermore, came to understand that Mr. S. had entered the office so excited and so preoccupied with his desire to share his good news about a job promotion that he had thoughtlessly tossed his coat. In turn, being understood allowed Mr. S. to arrive at an important awareness: namely, that his excitement in wishing to be recognized led, at times, to careless and inappropriate behavior that other people sometimes found offensive.

The following vignette illustrates another example of a patient feeling misunderstood when an intervention was made outside his experience.

During the middle phase of his treatment, a young man in his late teens would initiate each session with a quip or a joke. At the start of one particular session, as the patient glanced over at a plant hanging by the window, he laughingly commented, "What kind of plant is that, it looks sick!" The analyst, viewing himself as the target of the remark, interpreted the patient's comment as an expression of aggression displaced from him as the transference object onto the plant. The analyst's understanding followed his awareness of the patient's rage against his father, which had recently emerged in the treatment. The patient felt hurt by the intervention and countered by explaining that his jokes were not attacks but were, rather, his way of being close. He said, "I see these jokes as my being more comfortable with you and wanting to relate to you like a friend. This may sound strange, but this is the way I am with all my good friends and they with me. We're always kidding one another."

As the analyst shifted his attention to the "experience near" vantage point, he came to a new understanding of the meaning that joking held for his patient. Rather than an attack on the analyst as "target," his joking was a means of achieving closeness. In time the patient was able to uncover how his joking was a way of maintaining a relationship with his cold and distant father.

EMPATHY: SOME MISUNDERSTANDINGS

This process of thinking and feeling oneself into the inner life of another person can be open to a number of misunderstandings. First, we would like to emphasize that empathy is not a process

by which we guess, intuit, or magically perceive what is occurring in the mind of another. Second, empathy is not the same as
we might feel if we were in a similar situation. For example, the
therapist and patient may have experienced similar life circumstances. This does not mean, however, that the analyst's particular experience of that situation is the same as the patient's. The
following is an example of the analyst assuming that he knows
what the patient is experiencing because of having undergone a
similar life circumstance.

Mr. H., a depressed 25-year-old man with a serious self disorder, was
beginning to accomplish a number of his goals when his mother was
killed in an automobile accident. In the session following the accident
Mr. H. recounted the details of his mother's death with little emotion.
Having lost a parent in a similar way, the analyst assumed that his
experience had been like that of his patient. As Mr. H. spoke of the
accident, the analyst remembered with emotion the intensity of his
own loss and at one point responded with, "What a tragedy!" Immediately, Mr. H. lapsed into a long silence and then suddenly began
berating himself for not feeling the loss "as much as he should." This
led to an exacerbation of low self-esteem as he continued to compare
himself negatively to the analyst.

A third misunderstanding with regard to empathy is that,
whereas every sensitive analyst will experience concern with
whomever he or she works, placing oneself in another's experience does not mean becoming that person – that is, "taking over"
or "being flooded by," the patient's feelings. If, for example, this
same Mr.H. in a later session became suddenly saddened while
recounting the events of the funeral service, it would again be an
error of empathy if, through identifying with that feeling, the
analyst lost objectivity and began to commiserate with the
patient. That is, entering into and becoming a participant in the

sadness rather than being someone who understands the sadness can interfere with the analyst's ability to be objective and helpful. Finally, Kohut acknowledged that empathy per se may serve a secondary therapeutic function in that it can establish a meaningful supportive bond between patient and analyst. However, he also warned us that the use of empathy was not to be confused with "being nice" or "appearing sympathetic" or "curing through kindness." **He clearly stated that the primary function of empathy was to make possible the painstaking unfolding of a patient's inner experiences and the emergence of specific developmental needs (selfobject transferences).** It is this process that leads to in-depth understanding and interpretation, and to reliable psychological change. This in-depth empathic process led also to Kohut's theoretical formulations, and now opens the door for further advancements in theory.*

THE WIDER SCOPE OF EMPATHY

Kohut's view of empathy as the only way to understand the in-depth emotional life of another person is not unique to psychoanalysis. While we may not be aware of it, all of us to some extent place ourselves in the inner world of others in order to relate on a meaningful level. No matter what role we play in life, empathy remains the primary tool by which we come to understand and communicate effectively with others. For example, through empathy a mother comes to know and understand the emotional needs of her child. Similarly, a teacher is made aware

---

*There are those in the discipline of self psychology who take issue with the idea that the empathic process leads to the ongoing discovery and formulation of theory that further explains complex mental states (such as Goldberg 1988).

of the learning needs of the individual student, and a political leader is alerted to the human needs of his or her constituency. A judge relies upon empathy to understand opposing viewpoints.

DEVELOPING OUR POTENTIAL FOR EMPATHY

We recognize that certain individuals may possess a greater capacity for empathy than others. This does not mean, however, that empathy is an endowed gift bestowed on only a fortunate few. For Kohut has taught us that training and learning can make a difference in widening the range and scope of our basic capacity for empathy.

Perhaps more than anyone, the professional actor exemplifies Kohut's idea that training and learning can make a difference. It is well known that a serious actor who really wishes to "get into the shoes" of the character he is to portray – not merely to do an imitation of that character – will spend hours in training workshops to get a sense of what that particular character might experience in certain situations. To enhance this awareness the actor may travel to a particular geographic locale, read biographical works, examine photographs, and view films. These efforts help him gain access to a deeper, more accurate experience of how that character might think or feel.

Kohut's focus on the patient's subjective experience as the basis for understanding complex mental states is a clear directive for the analyst to develop his or her potential for empathy. This is not unlike the responsibility the serious actor assumes in discovering the inner life of a character. Of course, we recognize that an actor uses the discovery of a character's inner life for artistic purposes. On the other hand, an analyst uses the awareness of a patient's inner life for scientific purposes; that is, for understanding and explaining in the treatment situation.

Kohut has not spelled out ways to expand our scope of empathy through training and learning beyond the traditional avenues of personal analysis, clinical supervision, and general psychoanalytic study. He has, however, presented us with theories of the self that have broadened our psychoanalytic perception of heretofore unnoticed psychic configurations. It is to these theories, which emerged from Kohut's empathic immersion into the inner life of his patients, that we now turn in the following chapters.

CHAPTER 3

The Selfobject Concept and Selfobject Transferences

We have examined empathy and its vital importance to the self psychological observer, and we have taken a glimpse at Kohut the man and what inspired him to introduce his theory of the self. Now we return to the clinical setting, and attempt to reconstruct the steps that Kohut took to arrive at his conceptualizations. In particular, in this and the following chapter, we examine the concept of selfobject and selfobject transferences.

It should be emphasized that Kohut's theoretical considerations grew out of his attempts at understanding the mental life of his patients from the vantage point of their experience. Only through vicariously putting oneself in the shoes of the patient can one truly understand the experience of the patient and begin to construct a truly psychological theory to explain his or her behavior. Theories that explain behavior in psychobiological terms (drives, brain chemistry, and so on) or psychosociological terms (dependence, adaptation to reality, and so on) are removed from the area of the individual's experience and are, therefore, "experience-distant" theoretical constructions.

A full appreciation of the theory of self psychology, therefore, requires our reader to assume a similar experience-near vantage point, to walk in Kohut's shoes for awhile, so that the reader can think along with him in the formulation of his new theories.

This is an obviously difficult task. No one appreciated more than Kohut the challenge of opening oneself to new understandings. His own experience taught him that we are creatures of habit, clinging tenaciously to the old and familiar and resisting at all costs the new and different. It was his sensitivity to the threat that change represented that caused Kohut to move slowly not only in introducing his ideas, but also in translating these ideas into a language of the self that was different than what had been traditionally spoken in analytic circles. Not until 1977, with the publication of *The Restoration of the Self*, did he provide an alternative view of the traditionally accepted model or paradigm of the mind known as the "structural theory" (id, ego, and superego), and propose his complementary theory and language of the self. In this, self was considered as supraordinate – that is, as having its own center of initiative, independent of other agencies of the mind. No longer was the self considered only a self-concept or a content of the mind (self in the "narrower sense") as originally conceptualized by Hartmann (1950).*

---

*See Paul H. Ornstein's excellent delineation of three stages of Kohut's thinking in arriving at this conceptualization (1978, pp. 94–98).

Kohut stated in his introduction to *The Restoration of the Self:* "The emphasis of the present contribution is on . . . the psychology of the self in the broader sense – on a psychology, in other words, that puts the self at the center, examines its genesis and development and constituents, in health and disease" (Kohut 1977, p. xv).

COMING TO THE SELFOBJECT CONCEPT

With the preceding in mind, let us now address the primary concept of this chapter: namely, understanding and explaining the selfobject concept. As was previously noted, when Kohut had been confronted with a significant number of patients whose analysis of infantile conflicts had foundered, he began to wonder about the very theoretical assumptions that were the foundation of his own clinical approach.

From the experience-near vantage point, he made three observations. First, he was aware that his empathic immersion into the patient's experience provided him with a different understanding of the patient's mental life. When he communicated his understanding, the patient experienced being understood. Frequently, he or she experienced immediate relief and a feeling of well-being.

Secondly, Kohut realized that whenever he moved away from his empathic treatment stance, using interventions removed from his patient's experience, the patient reacted with disappointment, disillusionment, and rage. Kohut was aware that his experience-distant interventions had interfered with the understanding that was taking place.

His third observation helped solidify his thinking about the importance of understanding the patient from the experience-near vantage point. When Kohut returned to his experience-near empathic treatment stance and related to the experience of being misunderstood, the patient frequently regained a sense of well-being and relief. Repeated observations of a similar sequence of responses in these patients led Kohut to draw certain conclusions. He realized that within the therapeutic dyad he was not exclusively a "blank screen" transference figure – a target – upon whom the patients could displace infantile conflicts of a sexual and aggressive nature from significant earlier figures. He concluded that within the context of the empathic treatment bond that was established, he was providing a vital psychic function and that his patients were experiencing him as a needed extension of their selves.

Kohut introduced the term selfobject (1971) to denote one's experience of another as a part of the self. He likens the self's essential lifelong need for selfobjects, and for the functions they provide, to the body's demand for oxygen. In other words the self, in health or illness, can neither survive nor thrive without them. The nature of the particular psychological functions provided by the selfobject was eloquently described by Kohut (1984) in a letter to a friend:

> Throughout his life a person will experience himself as a cohesive harmonious firm unit in time and space, connected with his past and pointing meaningfully into a creative-productive future, [but] only as long as, at each stage in his life, he experiences certain representatives of his human surroundings as joyfully responding to him, as available to him as sources of idealized strength and calmness, as being silently present but in essence like him. . . . [p. 52]

Kohut recognized that selfobjects served psychological functions that are essential to all human experience, including the interpersonal, familial, social, cultural, and religious. For example, each spouse serves a selfobject function for the other. As well, mutual selfobject functions are provided by the parent and the child, the employer and the employee, the political leader and the elector-ate. Similarly the godhead serves a selfobject function for the believer. It can be emphasized that **a selfobject is the function that is usually provided by a person rather than it being the person** (Wolf 1988).

Of course, Kohut's awareness of the wider application of this concept derived from his in-depth observations in the clinical setting. Ongoing and prolonged immersion in his patient's experience sensitized him more and more to the various selfobject needs as they were expressed toward him in the transference.

CONCEPT OF THE SELFOJBECT TRANSFERENCE

As previously mentioned, Kohut's conception of transference was different from the usual understanding of transference: ". . . the tendency of the repressed infantile drive, which is attached to old objects, to seek new objects in its search for satisfaction" (Kohut 1951, p. 163).

It was Kohut's difficulty in reconciling the traditional under-standing of transference with his own clinical observations that ultimately caused him to reconsider both his concept of transfer-ence and his entire theoretical base. Thus, he soon learned that to his patients he was not a figure or "object" from the past who could be loved or hated for himself as a separate psychic entity. Rather, he became aware that he was being experienced as a ". . . direct continuation of an early reality that was too distant, rejecting or too unreliable to be transformed into solid psycho-logical structures" (Kohut 1959, p. 219).

Thus, for Kohut, transference was understood as selfobject transference (1977) (earlier he had defined this as "narcissistic transference" [1966, 1968, 1971]). As his patient's selfobject needs emerged in the treatment, Kohut was able to differentiate and identify three separate configurations: the *idealizing selfobject* transference, the *mirror selfobject* transference, and the *twinship selfobject* transference. (It was not until the publication of *How Does Analysis Cure?* [1984] that the twinship transference* was postulated as a separate configuration. Previously, the twinship selfobject transference was seen as a stage of the mirror transference.)

Furthermore, Kohut began to discern the various constitutional and environmental factors which interfered with the unfolding of these selfobject needs and, thereby, interfered with the development of the self. Ultimately, Kohut came to discern three unmet selfobject needs in his patients. We will discuss the idealizing and mirroring needs in this chapter. The third, twinship needs, will be taken up in the following chapter.

Thwarted Idealizing Needs: Searching for a Perfectionistic Image

Through his method of thinking and feeling his way into the patient's experience, Kohut became aware that patients who suffered rejection of their attempts to idealize their parents continued to long for a perfectionistic image of them, and tended throughout life to search for someone who could fit this unfulfilled and primitive picture.

An instance of this search is seen in the following: Ms. K. a 42-year-old respected book editor with a major publisher, entered treatment with one of the authors. She was concerned about her recent plans for marriage. She explained that she had been engaged on three previous occasions but had broken each engagement only days before the planned ceremony. She was worried that she would break off her

---

*Occasionally, we use the terms transference and selfobject transference (mirror, idealizing, and twinship) interchangeably for ease in writing.

current plans for similar reasons. These centered on her fears of making the wrong choice. Perhaps if she waited she would find someone who would be better for her. Upon each engagement she had tried to put these thoughts out of her mind, but was unable to do so. She had become obsessed with some flaw in each fiancé's appearance or personality. One fiancé had seemed at times to speak too loudly and occasionally upset her when he used imperfect grammer. Another was not as professionally ambitious as she would have liked him to be. At times, she felt that her current fiancé was not as intelligent as she. She had experienced this same feeling with the previous fiancés.

In time, as Ms. K.'s needs emerged within the idealizing selfobject transference, she was able to successfully work through her longing for the perfect mate and the many childhood traumas which had led to her fixation. The treatment of a patient (Ms. O.) with similar idealizing needs is discussed in detail in Chapter 12.

Thwarted Mirroring Needs: Two Defensive Outcomes

Kohut found that patients who underwent continuous rejection of their proud feelings of accomplishment, importance, and grandiosity as children, remained fixed on what he has termed a primitive grandiose self. Furthermore, he recognized that this fixation can result in two different defensive outcomes. First, this primitive self can become repressed and therefore hidden from consciousness, which can result in a "horizontal split" in the psyche (1971). In this case, the person negates his or her grandiosity and usually experiences low self-esteem, little enthusiasm for work or play, and vague depression.

[For example, Ms. G.,] a 31-year-old Hispanic woman, came into treatment because she was feeling depressed and hopeless about her future as a sculptor. Ms. G. remembered that as a child her favorite activity was molding objects from sand and clay. While her mother and father and two older siblings were generally appreciative of her talent, Ms. G. thought that no one really took her seriously. Many times her mother and father would openly discourage her by pointing out that other activities were more important. Ms. G. began to feel she had to hide her interest in sculpting from her parents. During high school she gave up her interest altogether. When she immigrated to the United States, at the age of 20, she met some artists who became her friends and encouraged her to continue sculpting. She took her friends' advice and for the first time began to take courses in sculpting. Whereas Ms. G. was praised by her instructors, and had been offered opportunities to show her work, she thought her art to be inferior. She was certain that she would be humiliated and accused of being a "fraud" if she were to exhibit her work.

In the course of her treatment, Ms. G. was able to understand these fearful expectations as arising from multiple traumatic rejections of her early expressions of grandiosity that had extended beyond the area of art. At the same time Ms. G. was able to risk the emergence of her previously repressed grandiose self, and eventually organized a number of exhibits of her work around the country.

Secondly, Kohut discovered that the primitive grandiose self can also be separated from consciousness through the mechanism of disavowal. This can result in what he had described as a "vertical split" in the psyche. These individuals, unlike the patient in the preceding case, have full expression of their primitive grandiose selves but are not aware of the consequences of these unmodified expressions. Their actions are usually seen by others as insensitive and uncaring.

[For example, Mr. B.,] a 30-year-old executive in a large brokerage firm, came into treatment upon the insistence of his wife who found his "arrogance" and "insensitivity" increasingly difficult to accept. She threatened to leave him if he continued to "take her for granted" and failed to carry through on his many agreed-upon commitments. In treatment Mr. B. initially thought his wife was unfair and was deliberately attempting to undermine his professional activities and success. Why should she complain if he forgot appointments with her or occasionally forgot her birthday or their anniversary? Eventually, Mr. B. came to see that his powerful grandiose feelings had a "life of their own" and were disconnected from his awareness of the meaning of his actions to others.

CHAPTER 4

Stages in the

Development of the Self

Through the observation of growth in his adult patients and the reconstruction of their early needs, Kohut came to understand that the idealized, mirroring, and later twinship selfobjects were a vital and necessary part of the self's development. Furthermore, he realized that within an optimally empathic milieu, the functions provided by those selfobjects would gradually become part of the self, leading to a more firm and stable self (structure), as well as an ongoing need for more mature selfobjects. However, he found that when the environment failed to provide these optimal circumstances, the self would become fixated at various stages of development.

EARLY DEVELOPMENTAL NEED FOR THE IDEALIZED SELFOBJECT

Very early merger experience with an all-powerful and comforting idealized parent figure provides the infant protection against overstimulation. If the mother or father are relatively free from problems that might interfere with their taking pleasure in their child, they can spontaneously respond to the child's joy as well as frustrations. As we are aware, infants shift from feelings of playfulness and excitement in one minute to fearful and frustrating feelings in the next.

The parent's empathic attunement (Beebe and Sloate 1982, Stern 1983) to these shifting states provides the means of understanding what the child's needs are, the immediacy of those needs, and what should be done to meet them. For example, the mother soothes the unhappy baby through gently and rhythmically rocking away its tension and tears. Simultaneously, she may softly whisper loving words or sing a lullaby – all the while looking into her baby's eyes and mirroring its looks, sounds, and changing responses to her. It is this experience, which Kohut describes as the merger experience with the strong, omnipotent idealized adult, that serves to protect the baby from too much frustration and stimulation and promotes the internalization of anxiety-relieving mental structures. The lack of internalization of these early anxiety-relieving functions can lead to diffuse and pervasive vulnerabilities later in life. Other theorists such as Elkisch (1957), Lichtenstein (1961, 1964), Mahler (1968), Meltzoff and Moore (1977), Sander (1962, 1964), and Stechler (1982) have also theorized that the beginning of the child's identity takes place through this merger experience which includes magnification and reduplication of shared affect states.

Kohut's discovery of these early selfobject needs has erroneously been taken by some to mean that self psychology focuses blame on the parents for their children's difficulties. It is important to clarify that Kohut is in no way implying that there should be a "perfect" mother. Rather, he states that the genesis of narcissistic vulnerabilities and fixations are best explained by the interplay between the inherited psychological propensities of the child and the personality needs of the parents. If the mother and/or the father are so absorbed in or preoccupied with their own unmet needs that they consistently fail to tune in to the child's, or to be appropriately responsive, then the child may remain fixated on his or her unmet early needs. An example of early idealizing needs is seen in the following brief vignette.

Miss C., 14 years old, was referred by her mother who discovered she had been smoking marijuana daily for a period of approximately one year. During this time the girl had neglected her studies and often overslept and was late for school. While she was getting passing grades, they were considerably lower than those of the previous year. During therapy it was learned that Miss C. had been a model child. She was an only child whose parents had showered her with presents, sent her to private school, and in every way attempted to encourage her in pursuing such activities as going to camp, taking piano lessons, and the like. Miss C.'s parents were professional writers who traveled widely after Miss C. was born. At times they took their infant daughter with them on trips but more often left her in the care of friends or relatives. Miss C.'s mother had attempted breast feeding but found it unsettling and was unable to produce an adequate quantity of milk; the bottle was then used exclusively and for the most part was propped during feedings as Miss C.'s mother did not enjoy the closeness of the nursing experience. Miss C. could remember that when she would climb into her mother's lap or in some other way make overtures, her mother did at times respond affectionately. However, there was a feeling of something missing. She could only explain it as a feeling of emptiness that her daily marijuana smoking seemed to fill. It became understood during her therapy that in part the drug had provided a substitute for the early idealized merger relatedness and the internalization of anxiety-relieving psychic structures. Miss C.'s turning to daily drug use was precipitated by an increased level of anxiety which became diffuse and intolerable as she approached and entered adolescence.

LATER PREOEDIPAL NEED FOR THE IDEALIZED SELFOBJECT

Later preoedipal disturbances in the idealized parent figure can prevent adequate internalization of drive-controlling, neutralizing, and channeling functions. This can lead to an intensification and sexualization of fantasies, ideas, and so on. The following brief vignette illustrates this disturbance.

Mr. D., 43 years old, came into treatment because his wife threatened to leave him if he did not get help to change his "insensitive" behavior toward her. An ad salesman for a large newspaper, he had been married twice previously and divorced each time after approximately two years. He had been married to his current wife for one year. Mr. D.'s major complaint was feeling sexually bored with his wives after a year or so even though he had had an extended sexual relationship with each of them before marriage. Mr. D. thought he had lost his sexual excitement with his wives because he felt trapped by the daily routine of married life. As time passed, his wives had come to seem more physically flawed. He could only break his sense of boredom by having extramarital affairs with more "perfect" women.

Mr. D. was an only child. He remembered that he had always been anxious and hyperactive. His mother and father were divorced when he was three, and he and his mother went to live with his maternal grandmother until his mother died when he was 5. He was then placed in a foster home, as his father refused to care for him and his maternal grandmother was unable to do so, having been ill for some time. He remembered having great difficulty concentrating in school and having to force himself to study. In spite of his efforts he got failing grades in both elementary and high school. In time Mr. D. was able to get in touch with his childhood deprivations and to share these experiences in treatment. The separation of his parents, the death of his mother and his subsequent placement in a foster home halted the process of idealization and of the internalization of anxiety-relieving and drive-channeling functions. As treatment continued, the idealizing transference emerged and the unfinished business of internalization of the functions of the idealized parent began to take place.

NEED FOR IDEALIZED SELFOBJECTS IN THE OEDIPAL STAGE AND BEYOND

If the disappointment occurs within the later preoedipal or oedipal period, then the child's internalization of parental value systems can be disrupted; this can lead to defects in the formation of the superego or conscience. The unmet need for this level of idealization can lead to the searching for idealized parental figures who can provide direction and guidance. Kohut gives an example of a patient who was overly strict with himself and his children (1984, pp. 155–156). The patient's father had died when the boy was 11. As a result, the idealization process had been interrupted at the critical developmental time during which parental values and standards are being internalized. Throughout life he had searched for idealized selfobject father figures to provide the missing parental guiding function of the father. During those intervals when this patient was without these selfobject connections or bonds, he was harsh and punitive to himself and his family.

The despair and depression that often follow severe disappointment during adolescence – such as disillusionment with an idealized figure – is well known. Severe disruption in the ongoing internalization process can leave the teenager bereft of idealized values and ideals. Hope for the future and for life itself can become diminished. It is also well known that suicides have occurred when teenage idols have died. Similarly, disappointments leading to despair at the ending of romantic relationships have resulted in many tragic adolescent suicides. Great numbers of teenagers have turned to peer groups, cults, drugs, and sexual promiscuity out of deep disappointment with parental figures, disappointment that can be generalized to include disillusionment with the norms of the society and with the political system.

DEVELOPMENTAL NEED FOR MIRRORING

Kohut's capacity for putting himself in his patients' shoes made it possible for him to recognize their unmet developmental need for confirming and validating mirroring responses. As previously noted in Chapter 1, Kohut became aware of the need for mirroring in his treatment of Miss F. He vividly described (1968, 1971) this 25-year-old patient who as a child had been deprived of the accepting, approving, and confirming responses she needed from her mother, who was depressed during several periods in the course of Miss F.'s childhood. Whenever Miss F. had expressed her needs for recognition and attention, her mother would deflect the attention to herself. Miss F., therefore, as a result of the successive rejections of her childhood exhibitionistic and grandiose expressions, remained fixed or arrested on these early strivings of the self. Kohut was able to recognize and appreciate Miss F.'s need for him to listen carefully, and her need for him to recognize and acknowledge the specific meaning and importance of what she said. Needs for the acknowledgment, understanding, and reflection of what is communicated were theorized by Kohut as selfobject mirroring needs expressed in treatment as the mirror selfobject transference. **He defined that sector of the self which strives to be assertive, expressive, and exhibitionistic as "the grandiose self."**

EARLY NEED FOR A MIRRORING SELFOBJECT

Kohut discovered that the grandiose self can emerge in three forms. In the most primitive form, the patient experiences the analyst as an extension of the grandiose self. Kohut gives an example of a patient, Mr. E. (1971, pp. 130–132), who, during times of separation from the analyst, would engage in a number of perverse activities. These included voyeuristic gazing at other men in public toilets, which provided the experience of being merged with or part of the other person. Kohut defines this experience as the revival of early stages of primary identity, a revival which occurs as a consequence of an insufficiently developed grandiose self.

The following patient was similarly deprived of early merger experiences. This patient required constant validation that he existed.

Mr. A., 23 years old, came into treatment because he was failing his university studies in engineering. He complained that he felt extremely pressured by the amount of academic work required.

As an only child, he had lived on his own since the divorce of his parents when he was 16 years old. He described himself as always having been anxious and on edge, even as a child. Mr. A. was highly agitated when he began treatment. He was concerned that treatment would entail his lying on the couch where he would not be able to see the analyst's eyes and, therefore, would "fade away" without the needed validation of being seen. Mr. A. thought he could feel comfortable with people only if he was able to look into their eyes. He remembered his interest in observing the eyes of people in photographs and magazines and on television. As far back as he could remember it seemed his parents would avert their eyes from his when speaking with him. How lonely and anxious he felt at those times – as if he were not there.

Mr. A. experienced a similar sense of anxiety, loneliness, and "not being there" when he had to spend hours of study time in the school library or alone at his desk at home. It especially disturbed him to see people happily involved in their studies. At these times his feeling of isolation became unbearable, and he would leave what he was doing and search for someone who would speak with him for long periods of time. It was only then that he could return to his studies.

NEED FOR TWINSHIP SELFOBJECT

In the second form described by Kohut, the grandiose self can emerge in the transference as a twinship with the analyst. Like the merger stage, twinship (or alter ego) is also a developmental stage of the self. This is a stage at which the child between the ages of 4 and 6 feels a likeness and sameness with a parent, usually of the same sex. Dressing up like Mommy or Daddy is a stage of the development of the self which is familiar to all of us. Children around this age also have imaginary friends or animals which are like-minded companions. Kohut (1971) had included this stage as one of the stages in the development of the grandiose self as manifested in a form of the mirror transference. Later, as we have indicated, Kohut (1984) suggested that twinship may well have its own developmental line which extends throughout life. For example, it is known that successful friendships and marriages require a substantial degree of thinking alike – that is, having similar ideas, values, and goals. These are especially important in the rearing of children. Otherwise, children understandably can become confused and emotionally torn by the divisiveness which inevitably is communicated. Twinship bonds are also especially important later in life when a person retires and the need for companionship is strong.

Kohut (1984, pp. 195-197), in his work with a female patient, describes the transference of an early twinship experience. This woman became preoccupied with covering the tops of containers during a period preceding Kohut's planned summer vacation. The patient associated to a memory of the loneliness she had felt when she was 6 or 7. At that time her relationship with her grandmother was disrupted when she and her parents moved away. Her grandmother had provided a warmth and closeness that she could not get from her parents. She began to imagine that a little girl, like her, lived in a bottle which she kept closed on her bureau. Her "genie in the bottle" was her twin to whom she would talk when she was lonely. In treatment, the revival of that twinship relatedness with her childhood imaginary twin – as currently played out by her placing covers on containers – was precipitated by the imminent separation from her analyst. The comforting experience of this symbolic reenactment offset the loneliness she anticipated, just as her twinship relatedness with her "genie" had offset the loneliness when she separated from her grandmother.

The following is an example of a patient whose early level of twinship relatedness had sustained him throughout a severely traumatic childhood, but had become limiting as an adult.

Mr. N., 25 years of age, sought treatment when he was unable to finish his undergraduate studies. He was considered by his friends to be a "professional student" in that he would take a variety of elective courses which had little to do with his major and for which he did not get credit toward his degree. He either avoided or delayed taking required courses and frequently did not complete them.

Mr. N. thought he should finish his studies as he wished to get married and begin a life outside of school. He was feeling pressure from his fiancée, who wished him to finish. He was also in debt and was financially pressured to get a job.

As treatment proceeded Mr. N. became aware of what the significance of being a student was for him. He associated back to those pleasurable times when his father had taught him to read and told him about the importance of learning. He had looked forward to learning new words each day. He remembered the many times his father took him to the library beginning when he was around 4. His father would point out the many books and tell him how many wonderful stories there were to read. It seemed that those had been the happiest times of his childhood. Other times, however, seemed to have been frightening and unhappy for him. His older sister took sides with his mother against his father, and because he had had a number of business losses she accused him of being irresponsible and a failure. Mr. N. remembered how, as a child, he would go to his room and "bury his head" in his books to avoid being disturbed by the relentless arguments. He came to realize how being a student and not graduating maintained a form of the twinship bond that he had had with his father. This provided him with warmth and recognition that sustained him throughout his development. Graduating meant moving away from his twinship bond and "going out into the world," where he was faced with asserting himself and competing to get ahead in the job market. Mr. N. had for the most part been deprived of the recognition and validation of his ability to be assertive and to implement his ideals and goals. While his father was able to meet Mr. N.'s needs within the context of twinship, the father, as a result of his own fears and anxieties about being assertive, was unable to recognize and appreciate his son's capacities for exhibiting strength and assertiveness, and for carrying out and completing tasks and goals. As a consequence, Mr. N.'s studies, like his father's, had no broader purpose than the experience of studying as an activity. As Mr. N. began to explore his need to maintain a twinship relatedness, which emerged as the initial or primary form of the selfobject transference with the analyst, he suffered considerable anxiety that he eventually analyzed and worked through.

LATER NEED FOR THE MIRRORING SELFOBJECT: MIRROR TRANSFERENCE IN THE "NARROWER" SENSE

As this working through continued, a secondary selfobject transference emerged in which Mr. N. slowly began to formulate specific goals and achieve them. The first of these goals that he achieved was the goal of graduating from college. The gradual emergence of Mr. N.'s assertiveness, assuredness, and ability to express his thoughts and ideas forward is what Kohut describes as the most mature form of mobilization of the grandiose self. Kohut defines this selfobject transference or bond as the mirror transference in the "narrower" sense, which is the reinstatement of that normal developmental stage at which children display to parents their budding abilities to run, play, jump, draw pictures, speak "big words," and so on. It is at this stage that children need and seek from their parents validating responses that they really are what they feel themselves to be. The parent's approving look, smile, or nod of recognition is the mirror by which children come to know that they are beloved. If parents have experienced rejection of their own childhood display of exhibitionism, they may have some difficulty in appreciating and mirroring their children's expressions. They may be unaware that their children's spontaneous desire for approval triggers associations to their own painful childhood feelings of rejection, when their own desires to be recognized were unsatisfied. Consequently, they may, in order to avoid any reminder of their traumas, ignore their children at these times or in some way show disapproval. As previously stated, repeated rejections in the face of early needs can lead to fixations or arrests of those needs. As adults such people may repress (horizontal split) their wishes and impulses to be assertive and exhibitionistic, as was the case of Ms. G. (Chapter 3); or they may give expression to them outside their awareness (vertical split), as was the case of Mr. B. (Chapter 3).

These case examples have been presented to highlight specific selfobject transferences that emerge in the treatment due to unmet childhood needs. It should be emphasized, however, that various forms of the mirror selfobject transference may emerge in different ways depending on the developmental level at which the fixations occurred.

MOBILIZATION OF THE GRANDIOSE SELF IN TREATMENT

Specifically, Kohut (1971, pp. 133–142) discussed three ways in which the mobilization of the grandiose self occurs in treatment: primary, reactive, and secondary. First, the primary mirror transference may arise directly from that point at which there was an arrest in the selfobject development. Kohut describes this as primary simply because it emerges first in the treatment. This development was evident in the case examples of Mr. A. (merger), Mr. N. (twinship), and Ms. G. (mirror transference in the narrower sense).

Second, the emergence of the grandiose self also occurs as a defensive reaction to disappointment with the analyst. Kohut defines this type of emergence as the reactive mobilization of an archaic self-image that is normally associated with various defensive expressions such as hostility, coldness, sarcasm, and silence.

The following is an example of one of the many occasions during a period of treatment with Mr. D. in which he retreated from an idealizing selfobject transference to a defensive reactive mobilization of the grandiose self. This usually occurred when he felt misunderstood, but in this instance it was precipitated by his consideration of the important developmental step of fathering a child. The way the analyst dealt with this defensive mobilization is also highlighted.

As previously described in this chapter, Mr. D. suffered the loss of his idealized mother, father, and grandmother. He was left with an early and primitive childhood longing for the perfect parental figure, and became dissatisfied with his wives as they came to seem "imperfect" and sexually boring. His early idealizing needs were mobilized in the course of his treatment. He began to establish a primitive form of idealizing selfobject transference with the "perfect" selfobject analyst.

As the idealizing selfobject transference continued to develop, Mr. D. frequently anticipated some disaster such as the analyst leaving or dying. At times he seemed thoroughly convinced that the analyst was untrustworthy and dishonest.

As Mr. D.'s search for perfection and his multiple past experiences of loss, despair, and hopelessness were analyzed, he became less obsessed with his thoughts of perfection. He had maintained his marriage, and was considering plans with his wife to have a child. In one particular session during this period Mr. D. became aware that his thought of fathering a child was a major step in "trust." He wondered if his wife would leave him and take the baby. He could anticipate this happening at the moment he would finally be happy and trusting as a husband and father. Although Mr. D. was able to understand his fearful anticipation as a revival of familiar childhood traumas, and although by the end of the session he was relieved by the analyst's empathic acknowledgment of the intensity of his anxiety, Mr. D. did not appear for his next session.

During the time scheduled for his session, however, he telephoned, and in a cold and distant manner reasoned that the analyst was leading him into disaster and that it was time to stop treatment and leave his wife. If he were to continue treatment and his marriage, he said, he would have to rely on the analyst for even greater understanding and trust. Mr. D. now seemed more cold, determined, and aloof as he expressed his conviction that no one was capable of that. The analyst was sensitively aware that Mr. D. was experiencing powerful feelings of mobilized reactive grandiosity which did not seem open to discussion – especially on the telephone. The analyst was also aware of an aspect of Mr. D.'s present experience that seemed to be evidence of the idealized selfobject transference bond that had been established during the course of the treatment. That is, the analyst sensed that Mr. D. was, with some difficulty, expressing a wish to reveal his interest in having the analyst understand why he did not attend the session.

When Mr. D. had finished his explanation, the analyst said that he appreciated his calling and helping him understand. The analyst also added that he recognized that it was not easy for Mr. D. to let people in on his ideas when he felt strongly about them. Mr. D. agreed, and, as a result of his feeling understood, his reactive grandiosity subsided and he began to reconsider his decision. By the end of the conversation it was agreed that he would speak further with the analyst and attend his next scheduled session.

Third, the mirror transference can evolve after a brief period of idealization. Kohut defined this type as a secondary mirror transference. The initial idealization of admired figures may arise in the patient's dreams, or there may be a direct expression of admiration for the analyst. This particular sequence is important in that it represents the transference repetition of what took place in the past. Kohut (1971, pp. 139-140, 242-259) gives an example of this sequence.

Mr. K., an industrial engineer in his early forties, initially developed a brief idealizing transference and then a secondary mirror transference. The idealization represented an attempt he had made at 3½ years old to idealize his father, after his mother had become severely critical and rejecting of him following the birth of his younger brother. His father, however, had been emotionally unable to accept his son's developmental need to glorify him, and rejected his son's attention. The son's idealization process was therefore cut short as a result of his traumatic disillusionment with his father. He retreated back to his primitive grandiose self which had been admired earlier by his mother. Mr. K. continued to pursue exhibitionistic activities into his adult life at the expense of other levels of self-development. During later stages in the treatment, when a brief idealizing transference precedes a mirror transference, the idealizing transference may emerge again as a secondary idealizing transference.

Another variation in the sequence of the development of the mirror transference may be the emergence of an idealizing transference after the establishment of a primary mirror transference.

II

Treatment in Self Psychology

CHAPTER 5

Transmuting

Internalization

Thus far we have touched on the role of empathy in everyday life as well as in the treatment situation. The concept of selfobject has been clarified, and examples of the various forms and sequences of the selfobject transferences have been illustrated. In this section we discuss treatment in self psychology, beginning with the process of transmuting internalization and the two-step therapeutic unit of understanding and explaining. First, however, we elaborate further on the concept of the supraordinate self.

THE SUPRAORDINATE SELF

The self can now be conceptualized as a tripolar entity consisting of the grandiose self sector, the idealizing sector and the twinship sector. As previously indicated, the self is considered supraordinate in that the emphasis is on the functioning of its parts as a cohesive whole. Its parts and functions are built into the self. In other words, the self is more important than and transcends the sum of its parts (Kohut 1975a, p. 749; 1977, p. 97). If children have not been too severely traumatized and have been able to establish the needed idealizing, mirroring, and twinship selfobjects,then development can progress toward the fulfillment of their creative potential or what Kohut defined as the "nuclear program of action" (1984, p. 10). As adults, these individuals would be able to utilize their unique talents and skills to pursue and implement mature ambitions and idealized goals with enthusiasm and a minimum of anxiety.

Thus Kohut theorizes that the self functions as a whole. This is in contrast to other psychoanalytic theories which see the self as the content of the mind (i.e., self-representations). The wholeness of the self is maintained through the interrelationship of its sectors or poles. This relationship is defined analogously in electrical terms as a "tension gradient" (Kohut 1977, p. 180). The psychological activity between these poles is defined as a "tension arc" (1977, p. 180; 1984, p. 4). It is this psychological activity which carries us forward to complete our development and actualize our potential. It is ". . . the dynamic essence of the complete, nondefective self . . . " (Kohut 1984, pp. 4-5).

TRANSMUTING INTERNALIZATION

Kohut has made it clear that our need and search for satisfying selfobjects continues throughout life. If our needs and attempts have been severely thwarted and defects in the self have occurred, we will attempt to sustain ourselves through various levels of regressive retreats. As indicated in the preceding examples, the depth of the regression depends on the overall severity of the trauma, at what developmental level the trauma occurred, and the extent of the damage to the self. **It is the inherent impetus to go forward in one's development that makes treatment possible even in the more serious disorders of the self.** This inherent impetus does not mean that patients come into treatment bright-eyed and happy to begin. It does mean, however, that there is a need within us to grow, a need that, even if dormant, can be reactivated through treatment.

As already noted, the selfobject transference and the way in which it emerges in treatment is determined by both the nature of the defect in the self and the sequence of the childhood traumas.

Before discussing the specific aspects of the treatment, it is important first to examine the growth-producing process that treatment is designed to bring about. This process is defined by Kohut as "transmuting internalization" (1971, 1977, 1984). It is the process by which patients can begin internalizing specific functions and accruing structures previously missing in their development. These self-validating functions are integral to maintaining confidence and self-esteem as well as to fostering the motivation and determination to carry out satisfying goals. The anxiety-relieving and self-soothing functions provided by the idealized selfobject are integral to the establishment of ideals, values, and goals, as well as to enabling people to direct their energies in a balanced way with neither too much nor too little stimulation.

Kohut (1971) points out three factors in the process of "transmuting internalization": First, the mental development must have reached a maturational level at which internalization of specific introjects (identifications) can take place. Secondly, if the frustration or disappointment with the object is optimal (optimal frustration), then the child can experience the inevitable disappointments in the idealized parent in a tolerable step-by-step way. If, on the other hand, there is a sudden and total disillusionment with the parent which, as previously stated, can result in fixations or arrests on early forms of idealized parental figures (imagoes), transmuting internalization is prevented. Such total disillusionment can be caused by excessive separations, permanent loss, or – the more common occurrence – a severe self disorder in the parental figure. This is discussed later. The third factor in the internalization process is the depersonalization of the internalized aspects of the parental figure, which involves the taking in of specific functions of the selfobject rather than gross identification with the selfobject. This internalization process leads to the formation of psychic structure that has been for the most part removed from the personality of the selfobject.

In his posthumous volume of 1984, Kohut further examined the question of the formation of psychic structure and transmuting internalization. He raised the following questions for further research:

1. Can reliable psychic functions be taken over from the selfobject directly, without going through the three-step process outlined here?

2. Can innate psychic functions be activated by the presence of the selfobject without the internalization of the functions of the selfobject?

3. Can one acquire psychic functions from the selfobject without preceding frustration?

4. How can we understand more clearly the shift from gross or total identification that occurs sometimes, as a result of a threatened or actual loss of the selfobject, to the gradual transmuting internalization of the functions of the selfobject?

Kohut asks two final questions: First, is there a decisive difference in the acquisition of psychic structure as an adult in psychoanalytic treatment, from the acquisition of psychic structure in the course of childhood development? And second, if such a difference does exist, of what does it consist?

Kohut's questions have alerted us to areas of future research that might broaden our general understanding of the development of the self, and inform us more fully about the specific effects the self-selfobject bond has on the moment-to-moment process of internalization of psychic structure.

THE THERAPEUTIC UNIT: UNDERSTANDING AND EXPLAINING

Kohut (1977, 1984) thought of the therapeutic process as consisting of two separate but interdependent steps. They are (1) *understanding* and (2) *explaining*. The understanding step involves the analyst's feeling and thinking his or her way into what the patient is experiencing in the moment and communicating in one form or another that the patient's experience has been grasped. This process allows the patient to feel understood. The experience-near empathic immersion into the experiences of the patient has been described in the chapter on empathy. It is the means by which an analyst can first gain access to, and come to an ongoing understanding of, the patient's inner world.

For example, if we return for a moment to Mr. S. in Chapter 2, we can see how the analyst's initial focus on the patient's action of tossing his rain-soaked coat on a newly upholstered chair led to an erroneous conclusion that the patient was angry. It was only after the analyst was able to immerse himself in the patient's experience that he was able to understand that the patient was feeling misunderstood and hurt, and later that his action was not directed toward the analyst. Rather, it was a thoughtless action resulting from the patient's enthusiasm about another matter. Here we have an example of how understanding, the first step of treatment, can come about only through the experience-near empathic approach.

Kohut has emphasized that understanding based on the empathic process is not to be confused with the analyst's being "understanding" in the sense of being "nice," "kind," "friendly," "warmhearted," and so on. Self psychology believes that the empathic experience-near mode of data gathering can bring about the deepest level of understanding complex mental states. **The empathic process is employed solely as a scientific tool to enable the analyst eventually to make interpretations to the patient that are as accurate and as complete as possible.**

The second step, explaining, is that phase of the treatment process whereby the meaning of the patient's experience is interpreted in dynamic, economic, and genetic terms and is the phase that brings about the psychoanalytic cure. Whereas the first step of the treatment process focuses on grasping the patient's experience and communicating **that** the experience has been grasped, this second step focuses on communicating the **meaning** of the patient's experience.

While certain patients may require long periods of understanding before being able to accept interpretations (the explanatory phase), both steps must eventually be taken to effect an in-depth level of understanding and with it substantial structural changes.

Verbal interpretations explain the current and past interrelationship of psychological processes, and, therefore, expand the patient's understanding on the dynamic, economic, and genetic levels. This step leads to a working through of the effects of childhood traumas, and facilitates the loosening of fixations and the development and solidification of new editions of selfobject transferences.

It should be emphasized that in each of the steps of understanding and explaining, no effort is made to satisfy the patient's need for direct gratification. For example, patients who have formed a mirror selfobject transference might wish the analyst to visit their homes or share in some event with which they are involved in order to show the analyst their accomplishments. Patients who have formed idealizing transferences may wish advice and guidance around specific issues from the "all wise" idealized analyst. Patients who are in a twinship transference frequently wish the selfobject analyst to be a friend and plan activities together.

Understanding and interpreting such wishes and needs rather than trying to directly fulfill them is necessarily depriving. However, if there is a balance between the patient's experiencing the anxiety-relieving empathic selfobject bond and experiencing deprivation, then the frustration remains at a tolerable level (optimal frustration). Transmuting internalization of the functions of the selfobject analyst and the building of self structure can then occur.

TYPES OF SELF STRUCTURE: PRIMARY AND COMPENSATORY

Kohut (1984) points out that there are many kinds of healthy selves and that the analytic route toward cure with anyone depends on each individual's unique potential for self development. The healthy self, no matter what its course of development, will consist predominantly of what Kohut has defined as primary and compensatory structures.

Primary structures are self structures that develop naturally over time according to one's particular endowment. If children have experienced at least reasonably sufficient empathic responses from their parents, and if the inevitable empathic failures by the parents have not been so severe as to produce fixations, there will be a progression in the development of the self-selfobject bonds, and thus structure building will take place through transmuting internalization.

Compensatory structures are self structures that are secondary in that these structures are formed as a result of some defect in the self. **By defect we are referring to inadequate internalization of the various functions in one or more of the three poles of the self.** These defects occur as a consequence of traumatic selfobject failures. Defects may occur throughout the development of the self as a result of disturbances ranging from those in the early developmental stages (primary disturbance), to those later disturbances in the oedipal development when there may be a firmly established self.

Compensatory structures are structures that make up for the structural defects in one pole of the self by a concentration of structural development in another pole of the self. For example, defects in the development of the grandiose self can occur if the child is severely and/or repeatedly traumatized when he or she attempts to get recognition for accomplishments, ideas, and the like. As a result of the unavailability of the mirroring selfobject, the child may develop a strong idealizing bond with a parental figure. The reverse may also occur. If the child experiences traumatic disappointment in the idealized figure, he or she may actively seek recognition from mirroring selfobjects. Of course, parental selfobjects must be available in order that there be an opportunity for adequate development of compensatory structure.

A child may develop compensatory structure in the twinship pole of the self if there are repeated failures by mirroring and idealizing selfobjects. Kohut's female patient, who as a child turned to her imaginary twin, the genie in the bottle, when she was forced to move away from her grandmother, is a good example. This can be seen as her effort to find a twinship selfobject, albeit an imaginary one, to fill the emotional void created by her distant and cold parents. Mr. N., as described earlier, found during his childhood a sustaining twinship related-ness with his father around studying and learning. The compen-satory structure-building in this sector of the self took place as a result of the repeated disillusionment with his mother and father in the idealizing sector, and the relentless arguments that severely inhibited the development of his grandiose self. Mr. N. was able to perform well as a student. He graduated from high school with honors and achieved good grades throughout college. However, he was able to achieve these successes only within the context of being a student – that is, as a student he could maintain a twin-ship relatedness as a predominant way of functioning. Thoughts of finally graduating and taking on responsibilities as a husband mobilized childhood traumas around being assertive and exhibi-tionistic. In treatment, expectations of inevitable failure emerged. Along with these expectations were the painful experiences of disillusionment with his intimidated and financially unsuccessful father. Mr. N. was able to substantially work through levels of these experiences; this allowed him in time to move from his predominant mode of twinship functioning to a more developed use of his grandiose self. Mr. N. graduated from college, secured a high-level administrative job, and received several promotions. He decided against marriage with the woman to whom he had previously been engaged, but eventually married a more compat-ible woman who was more appreciative of his developing skills and talents.

CHAPTER 6

Mental Health and Illness

In the preceding chapters we have discussed some of Kohut's primary conceptualizations, such as the selfobject, the selfobject transferences, and development of the self in treatment through the process of transmuting internalization. In this chapter we examine Kohut's concepts of mental health and illness.

Kohut views psychological health as the ability of an individual self to realize its own unique ". . . nuclear program in the course of its life's span . . ." (Kohut 1984, p. 42). He equates his own definition of what is normality in mental health to the definition of mental health

as described by C. Daly King, who thought that the average may
often be abnormal. The normal, on the other hand, can be
defined as that which functions in accordance with its design
(Kohut 1984, p. 212, note 1). The fundamental premise of this
definition is that each of us has his or her own unique endowment as well as direction for actualizing our inherent potential.

CRITERIA OF A HEALTHY SELF

Even though Kohut does not suggest definitive criteria by which
one can determine a "normal" or healthy self, he does suggest
throughout his writings certain attributes and capacities that
characterize a well-functioning individual. Important among
these criteria is the capacity for empathic attunement and the
curiosity and wish to understand the needs of others. Important
too is the ability to compromise and to delay satisfying one's
own needs when necessary in order to meet the needs of others.
Thus parents can feel confident and satisfied in their being
consistently sensitive to the needs of their children even when, at
times, doing so is burdensome and requires giving up previous
plans and goals. Couples can feel confident in their capacity to
meet each other's needs in a balanced way with a sense of
satisfaction and accomplishment. Individuals can feel secure in
their ability to relate sensitively to a variety of personalities,
thereby adding to the enrichment of their lives.

A further criterion of a developed self is being able to love.
Kohut states, ". . . the more secure a person is regarding his own
acceptability, the more certain his sense of who he is, and the
more safely internalized his system of values – the more self-
confidently and effectively will he be able to offer his love . . .
without undue fear of rejection and humiliation" (Kohut 1971,
p. 298).

Creativity is another indication of a healthy self. For Kohut this attribute may range ". . . from a new-found ability to perform a restricted range of tasks with zestful initiative to the emergence of brilliantly inventive artistic schemes or of penetrating scientific undertakings. . . ." (Kohut 1971, p. 308). He does not, however, restrict creativity to great scientific discoveries that are openly acknowledged or to artistic productions that are publicly acclaimed. On the contrary, he feels that the potential for creativity lies within every human being and encompasses a wide scope of human activities. He notes, "Unsolved intellectual and aesthetic problems, for example, create a narcissistic imbalance which in turn propels the individual toward a solution – be it now the completion of a crossword puzzle or the search for the perfect place for the new sofa in the living room. . . . The solving of the intellectual or aesthetic problem . . . always leads to a feeling of narcissistic pleasure, which is the emotional accompaniment of the suddenly restored narcissistic imbalance" (Kohut 1971, pp. 315–316).

Humor can be considered another criterion of a healthy self. Kohut, however, does not mean humor as the self-demeaning wit and biting sarcasm that bring laughter at one's own or another's expense. On the contrary, he characterizes humor as an ability to laugh good-naturedly at one's previously held self-importance or former fanatically held beliefs and values of a political, religious, or philosophical nature.

Wisdom is probably the most elusive of the attributes that characterize a healthy self. Its highest level of attainment, and one acknowledged by Kohut to be achieved by only a few rare people, is that of coming to terms with and accepting one's own finiteness and mortality. Yet Kohut felt that a modicum of wisdom is achieved by a far larger number of people when they come to grips with and accept joyfully their own personal limitations, the human frailties of their analyst, parents, as well

as the normal shortcomings of both the analytic process and their
own growing-up experiences. In speaking specifically of wisdom
Kohut (1971) emphasizes:

> The analyst should not aim, nor indeed expect, to achieve it;
> and we should not, by any pressure, be it ever so subtle,
> induce the analysand to strive for it . . . such pressures and
> expectations from the side of the analyst lead only to the
> establishment of insecure wholesale identifications, either
> with the analyst as he really is or with the patient's fantasy
> of the analyst, or with the personality which the analyst
> may try to present to the patient. [p. 327]

PSYCHOPATHOLOGY IN SELF PSYCHOLOGY

Kohut's thinking about what constitutes healthy functioning
and normalcy in development was derived from his understanding the pathology of his patients from the "experience-
near" vantage point. Thus Kohut has recognized that every
symptom and behavior finds its roots in an in-depth human
experience, and that these experiences are variations on a theme
of self-preservation and/or self-actualization. It is from this vantage point, when one allows oneself to enter into the subjective
world of another, that issues of psychopathology from a self
psychological point of view may be both experienced and appreciated. With this as a backdrop, Kohut offers the following
diagnostic categories.

First, he broadly distinguishes between secondary and primary disturbances of the self (Kohut 1977, pp.191–199). Secondary disturbances are the reactions of a firmly established self
to the usual experiences of life within the spectrum of success and
failure. The heightening and lowering of self-esteem, with the

self's accompanying reactions of rage, despondency, and hope, are part of everyone's normal reactions and are not necessarily pathological.

The primary disturbances of the self are subdivided according to a number of distinct psychopathological categories depending on the nature and severity of the disturbance. The first and the most severe are those which are traditionally referred to as the psychoses. Here the damage to the self is considered to be more or less permanent, and the threat of dissolution or fragmentation of the self is continuous. **This threat of dissolution or loss of the self is experienced by the individual in what Kohut has described as disintegration anxiety.** This is the deepest and most intense form of anxiety and may occur in all the self disorders should the structural integrity of the self be threatened. Kohut distinguishes this form of anxiety from what is commonly referred to as "castration anxiety," which is fear of being killed or mutilated because of one's incestuous longings. He also distinguishes disintegration anxiety from separation anxiety, which is the fear of the loss of an "object" or an important other.

The second subgroup among the primary self disturbances is that of the borderline states. In this category of disorders the damage to the self is also considered to be permanent; but in the borderline states, unlike the psychoses, the central defect of the self is covered over by an effective defensive structure that protects it against protracted fragmentation, severe depletion, and debilitating chaos.

The third subgroup, the narcissistic personality disorder, involves a far more flexible and resilient self than do the borderline and psychotic. In this disorder, reactions of enfeeblement and fragmentation are temporary rather than permanent. The self possesses a sufficient enough cohesion to form a selfobject transference with the analyst, and, therefore, this disorder is considered analyzable. Symptoms that characterize this level of self disorder are hypochondriacal complaints, feelings of depression, a lack of zest, and an extreme sensitivity to slights.

The fourth and final subgroup of the primary disturbances of the self is the narcissistic behavior disorder. In this disorder the symptoms of the breakup of the self are usually expressed through some form of "acting out" such as addictions and perverse or delinquent behavior. Kohut emphasizes that it is not only the assessment of the behavioral manifestations and symptoms that leads to a differential diagnosis. To clearly distinguish between the narcissistic behavior and personality disorders and the borderline and psychotic disorders, as well as between these and the neurotic personalities, one must also assess the nature of the transference. It is the eventual establishment of a stable selfobject transference which is the most significant and reliable indicator (1971).

Later secondary disturbances in the self can occur as a consequence of traumatic oedipal selfobject experiences. These disturbances can result in what is commonly referred to as the psychoneuroses. Some symptoms characteristic of this condition are anxiety, depression, phobias, obsessive thinking, and compulsive behavior.

ANALYZABILITY

Of the primary self disorders, Kohut felt that only the narcissistic personality and the narcissistic behavior disorders were analyzable. He believed that the other more severe self disorders were amenable to a more limited form of treatment through which a strengthening of old defensive structures and/or a building of new defensive structures could occur. Kohut (1971, 1984) reasoned that because of the severity of the damage to the self in those disorders, a workable selfobject transference which would necessarily loosen defenses against a fragilely held-together self would, at least in most instances, be intolerable.

At first glance one might surmise that Kohut's distinction of analyzability seems pessimistic regarding his prognostic outlook for the more severe self disorders. However, Kohut recognized that seriously disturbed patients might – depending on such circumstances as the personality and empathic capacity of the analyst – be able to establish a reliable and workable selfobject transference. He stated, "The line, as is generally true for the differentiation between neurosis and psychosis, is not an immovable one. It may depend, for example, on the skill and special gifts of the therapist or on the special psychological fit between a given patient and the personality of a given therapist" (Kohut 1984, p. 219, note 7).

To complement this statement, he also offers a moving clinical vignette of a borderline patient in which he attempts to demonstrate – through self-scrutiny and a genuine acceptance of the patient's reproaches against the therapist – that not all the patient's complaints are expressions of a negative transference. Rather, Kohut suggests, the patient may be reacting to the analyst's lack of understanding and unempathic interventions. In time, he says, the patient and the analyst might experience a crucial moment of understanding whereby a borderline patient may be able to begin to form an in-depth selfobject transference, which could make analysis possible. For those colleagues of his who saw these relentlessly negative patients as unanalyzable, Kohut remarked: "My inclination is to respond with the old adage that they should get out of the kitchen if they cannot stand the heat" (1984, p. 183).

THE ETIOLOGY OF SELF DISORDERS

Psychoanalytic and psychiatric case studies, as well as the commonly held cultural opinion regarding the origins of emotional disturbance, traditionally look to some particular event in early life to explain an individual's aberrant or pathological behavior. Depending upon which theoretical or philosophical model one employs in understanding behavior, explanations of psychopathology may range from "primal scene exposure," a sibling's birth, death, or illness, actual sexual seduction, to sudden separations or losses. All of these events are naturally recognized by self psychologists as having a deleterious and damaging effect on the self. Rather than viewing them, however, as the basis of disturbances, self psychology looks upon them as crystallization points signaling deeper causative factors–as, in other words, a grossly unempathic selfobject milieu. Kohut (1977) states:

> I believe that psychoanalysis will move away from its preoccupation with the gross events in the child's early life. There is no doubt that gross events . . . can play an important role in the web of genetic factors that lead to later psychological illness. But clinical experience tells us that in the great majority of cases it is the specific pathogenic personality of the parent(s) and specific pathogenic features of the atmosphere in which the child grows up that account for the maldevelopments, fixations, and unsolvable inner conflicts characterizing the adult personality. [p. 187]

Thus, for self psychologists, the origin of psychopathology is not so much a specific traumatic event or even a specific type of child-rearing philosophy. The major issue here is whether or not the parents have adequate self structure in their own development. It is the parents' security and self-confidence that allow them to meet their children's selfobject needs without resentment, and/or without the need to compete in some way with their children to satisfy their own unfulfilled needs.

If the parents' own narcissistic needs remain insufficiently fulfilled, this may lead to severe conflicts in the raising of their children. Fixations on primitive forms of selfobject configurations can occur as a result of chronic and traumatic deprivations. Kohut and Wolf, in their 1978 summarizing statement of the theory of self psychology, provide simple but poignant vignettes which exemplify the type of chronic interaction between a child and its selfobject parents that might eventuallylead to fixations in one or more poles of the self. **They caution their readers, however, not to view these instances as single events,but as characteristics of a chronic attitude on the part of the parental selfobjects.**

The first such vignette describes a young girl who eagerly shares a significant success of her own with her mother. The girl's enthusiasm is dampened, however, when the mother uses the opportunity to deflect away from her daughter's achievement to talk of her own early successes. The second vignette describes a boy who longs to hear about his idealized father's own past glory, the battles he had fought and won. The father is unable to accept his son's need to idealize him and cannot comply with the request. He feels threatened, embarrassed, tired, and bored, and then he leaves for the local bar where he finds some temporary relief from his own emotional deprivations, which were triggered by his son's idealizing needs.

TYPES OF SELF DISORDERS

Commonly encountered types of self disorders that result from the various developmental failures touched upon in the preceding section are described in brief by Kohut and Wolf (1978).* They believed that an overview of such syndromes might be useful to clinicians. This typology was not intended as a final and definitive classification but only as a broad clinical guideline. The authors also warn of attempting to find a neat and simple fit

---

*These types of self disorders are further exemplified by E. S. Wolf (1988).

between patient and syndrome. With certain individual personalities, one of these classifications might best describe the overall
state of the self. With others, two or more of these types might
apply at different times.

Understimulated Self

Individuals who have experienced severely depriving, nonmir-
roring responsiveness from the selfobject environment of childhood may present, in the clinical setting, a self that is noticeably
understimulated. They frequently complain of a lack of vitality
and of strong emotional responsiveness, a sense of inner dead-
ness, and a general mood of apathy and boredom. Other people
might also experience them in this way. To compensate for this
lack of inner excitement with the self, these individuals frequently resort to external sources of stimulation. For example,
children may employ rocking, head banging, compulsive masturbation, daredevil feats, possibly even suicidal activities. Adults
on the other hand, having a wider variety of activities to choose
from, may attempt to stimulate their deadened selves through
sexual promiscuity, perverse acting out behavior, hypersociabil-
ity, and/or addictive behaviors such as gambling or drug and
alcohol abuse. An "empty depression" lingering from the chron-
ically unresponsive selfobject milieu of the patient's childhood is
usually underlying all of these activities.

Fragmenting Self

Such a description captures at times the self of everyone from the
healthy to the most disturbed. For each of us has difficult days
when he or she feels at loose ends and nothing seems to have
gone right. Yet fragmentation as part of a narcissistic personality

disorder is experienced more acutely. For instance, it may be observed clinically with an individual patient who, though he normally dresses quite meticulously, may in one particular session present himself in a disheveled and poorly groomed state. The basis for such a condition might be associated with an emotional reaction to an unempathic experience in the treatment, in which the therapist failed to recognize a moment of exhibitionism when the patient reported a new insight or an important external success. A state of wholeness and well-being might quickly return, however, when the unempathic instance is identified, acknowledged, and its early roots analyzed. In the case of more severe narcissistic personality disorders the experience of fragmentation may be one in which there is a sense of the body breaking apart, or even a compulsive hypochondriacal worry about the condition of one's physical health. Though, in these instances, fragmentation experiences may exist for a more protracted period of time, self-cohesion will often return soon after an empathic bond is reestablished.

Overstimulated Self

This is an emotional state that results from an excessive or phase-inappropriate overstimulation on the part of the selfobjects toward the child's grandiose-exhibitionistic and idealizing poles of the self. For example, certain individuals who manifest this syndrome may easily become overexcited, which leads to an intense and crippling anxiety whenever their greatness fantasies are stimulated either by a public success or an outward recognition of their achievements. Consequently, much of the creative potential of these individuals remains unrealized because of the anxiety and fright that such stimulation causes the self. If it is predominantly the idealizing sector of the self that has been overstimulated by the selfobjects of childhood, because of the selfobjects' own needs for admiration and idealization, the resultant fixation might be an ongoing longing for merger and oneness with an idealized selfobject, a longing that will be so overstimulating that it could threaten the very equilibrium of the self. Because the mere presence of idealized selfobjects represents a threat, and therefore needs to be shunned, these individuals deprive the self of opportunities for expanding their capacity for healthy enthusiasm, both for admired others as well as for the values and goals that they represent.

Overburdened Self

This is the self that was not afforded the opportunity as a child to merge with the idealized selfobject, and that did not receive the necessary calming and soothing affective response in moments of intense emotion and spreading anxiety. Such experiences result in the self being overburdened, a condition which in turn brings about a perception of the world as both a hostile and dangerous place. In the therapeutic setting it is usually a narcissistic injury that breaches the self-selfobject bond between such a patient and the analyst, an injury of the type that has caused these individuals to experience the world in a suspicious and paranoid way. A calm, cohesive, and unburdened self may soon return when the self-selfobject bond is once again restored by a correct interpretation or intervention on the part of the therapist.

7

The Place of Drives in

Self Psychology

We now turn to how drives are understood within self psychology. We begin with a discussion of drives in classical psychoanalysis.

CLASSICAL PERSPECTIVE

Psychoanalysis from its inception has been based on a dual drive theory that maintains that the source of all human motivation is found in the biological determinants of sexuality and aggression. Freud's concept of drives has been the cornerstone of psychoanalysis. Disputes, disagreements, and eventual splits between Freud and many of his most well-known disciples (Jung, Adler, Rank, Horney, and others) centered upon this issue. Drives have been such a fundamental part of classical psychoanalysis that it has been commonly referred to as "drive theory." In later revisionist schools, drives have held a less prominent or even negligible role.

According to drive theory an infant is born into the world with a source of drive energy that is, during the progressive stages of development, increasingly processed and neutralized by a maturing psychic apparatus (id, ego, and superego). The ego (executive agency of the mind) and the superego (conscience) modify and channel the drives into useful activity and appropriate behavior. Freud acknowledged that the drives were not open to analytical investigation, but that they could only be observed in their derivative forms such as in fantasies, wishes, dreams, and symptoms. Yet Freud assumed that the drives found their origin in certain somatic sources (Freud 1915).

Within this theoretical frame the clinician regards his patients' psychological problems as neurotic conflicts; that is, as infantile instinctual impulses pressing for gratification but countered by the moral precepts of the superego and the defenses of the ego. This portrayal of human psychological disturbance is the heart of mainstream psychoanalysis. It is this theoretical model to which Kohut ascribes the title "Guilty Man," because classical theory depicts man burdened by guilt for his instinctually based incestuous wishes. Kohut's theory of the self attempts to address the inner emptiness of modern man as he struggles to find meaning and purpose to his life; Kohut refers to this model as "Tragic Man" (1977).

Classical psychoanalytic theory and technique emphasize helping the patient become aware of repressed sexual and aggressive impulses toward early incestuous "objects," within the context of a relationship in which the analyst is viewed as a separate and independent transference object. Of course, a major focus of the treatment is the analysis of the patient's defenses and resistances against the emergence of unacceptable aggressive and sexual impulses within the transference.

SELF PSYCHOLOGY'S CRITIQUE OF DRIVE THEORY

Kohut repeatedly expressed his concern that explaining complex mental states by means of experience-distant constructs such as the drives seriously limits understanding the individual patient. He was well aware that it is a natural condition for us all to have sexual and aggressive wishes, and, at times, to have lustful and even murderous impulses. Unlike the more traditional analytic focus on the harnessing or taming of these impulses through the treatment process, self psychology's focus is on understanding what it is like for these patients as they experience their wishes and impulses. It is only through an empathic immersion into the patient's experience that the analyst can understand the true psychological meaning that these experiences have for the patient.

Oedipus Complex

For example, let's compare the classical view of that which is considered a universal developmental complex of problems. We are referring to the Oedipus complex. Classical psychoanalytic theory assumes that every child has sexual feelings toward the parent of the opposite sex and rivalrous thoughts of getting rid of the parent of the same sex. As is well known, Freud introduced this concept in his *Interpretation of Dreams* (1900). The term Oedipus complex was taken from the Greek legend about Oedipus, who unknowingly killed his father and married his mother. With this complex of problems as a necessary and universal given, the classical analyst assumes that everyone seeking treatment would necessarily have problems with unresolved sexual and aggressive impulses at the level of his oedipal development. A focus of treatment, therefore, would be on exposing these drive impulses through the patient's associations and the analyst's interpretations.

Kohut, throughout his years of research in understanding his adult patients from the experience-near vantage point, did not find evidence of oedipal pathology in all of his patients. Based upon clinical evidence derived from the completed analyses of certain narcissistic personality disorders, he concluded that **the healthy child will enter the oedipal phase in a joyous manner and will experience pride in his or her developmental achievements if the parents can recognize and appreciate them.** The child's affectionate attitude does not have to disintegrate into fragmented sexual impulses as a result of unempathic and rejecting responses. In addition, he believed, the child's assertiveness does not have to turn into destructive hostility.

Therefore, Kohut considered the oedipal phase to be a normal part of development rather than an inevitable complex of problems. Only if there are disturbances in the selfobject milieu does one see evidence of hostility and intense sexual impulses. He referred to these manifestations as secondary symptomatic manifestations, symptoms not fueled by infantile drives as is viewed classically. For Kohut, the normal and healthy equivalent to what classical theorists consider to be the aggressive and sexual drives is assertiveness and affection.

Female Sexuality

Let's move now to another tightly held traditional concept in the development of the girl child. We are speaking here of the envy the little girl has of the boy's phallus. It is commonly, and somewhat pejoratively, referred to as "penis envy." According to the traditional theory, the young girl's early recognition of her lack of a penis is an inevitable narcissistic injury. Furthermore, the theory states that it is this inevitable injury that accounts for major disturbances of self-esteem found in women. Ultimately, as the little girl moves forward in her development, she identifies with the penisless mother. Her wish for a child is considered an expression of her desire for a phallus.

Kohut (1975b) agrees with the observation that every girl experiences, to a greater or lesser degree, an inevitable narcissistic injury with her early recognition of this physical difference. However, he seriously questions whether this phenomenon per se could account for the major disturbances of self-esteem in women or for the natural desire of women to bear children. On the contrary, Kohut believes that the healthy woman's wish to have a baby is the culmination of her feminine development. For example, expressions of the young girl's desire to be a mother, as manifested in creative play activities, are, to Kohut, evidence of a healthy sense of self. In this view, the later joyful wish of the grown woman to have a baby, or to express this desire in other creative activities such as her career, can also be a product of positive self-esteem.

But how does self psychology explain the frequently observed clinical fact, which is sometimes disguised and defended against, of the erotic desire of some women to have a male phallus?

Kohut disagrees with the belief that "penis envy," detected

in some women in analysis, is a universal expression of a biologically based narcissistic trauma that affects all women equally. Rather than an expression of "biological bedrock," Kohut considers it to be "psychological surface," covering a particular woman's enfeebled and depressed self. Her erotic fantasies of having a penis, or her desire to have one, is thus not an expression of an attempt to make up for a biologically based difference with men, but is evidence of a craving to fill in the psychic deficits that she suffered so pervasively at the hands of the unempathic selfobjects of her childhood. Having lost hope of ever attaining the responsiveness of those early mirroring selfobjects, or a merger with the idealized selfobjects, she may turn to erotic fantasies for self-stimulating and self-soothing sensation states that act as a substitute for the missing self structure.

It can be emphasized that these perverse sensation-producing fantasies and activities may temporarily stimulate the self, but they only substitute for self structure and, therefore, lead only to increased psychological addictionlike cravings.

Destructive versus Nondestructive Aggression

Classical psychoanalysis portrays aggression as a biologically based primal drive that eventually must be processed by the psychic apparatus and ultimately modified and channeled by the ego and superego. The treatment implication of this theoretical assumption is to bring about an exposure of the patient's aggression within the context of the transference. A patient who has difficulty expressing angry feelings, thoughts, or ideas may be described as having trouble managing his or her anger, or as tending to deny, suppress, or repress hostile angry feelings, thoughts, or ideas. While these descriptions may be criticized as oversimplifications and distortions of the classical theory, they do represent a not uncommon attitude that reflects that theory.

Thus we see that within this theoretical context it would be assumed that, as previously suggested, every patient would have problems with aggression as well as with sexuality. Kohut (1977) again takes strong exception to this basic premise of classical psychoanalysis. By his opposition, however, he is not denying the obvious phenomenon of hostile and destructive human impulses. On the contrary, he continues to maintain that the evidence for human destructiveness is indisputable. Therefore, for Kohut the extent and importance of this destructiveness is not in question; what is at issue is its significance and meaning to the individual.

Through his empathic immersion in his patients' experience, particularly in those instances in which there was extreme resistance to the analytic process, Kohut came to a different understanding of his patients' angry and hostile responses. Rather than viewing them as an expression of biological drives, he came to understand these expressions in much the same way as he understood perverse and erotic fantasies and activities – that is, as secondary reactions or "breakdown products" resulting from empathic disruptions of the self-selfobject unit. Thus, many of the angry and defensive responses of his patients that he had previously interpreted with theoretical certaintyas expressions of resistance against uncovering repressed material in the transference, were now acknowledged by him to be legitimate expressions of anger, at least partially induced by his own lack of empathic attunement to his patients' selfobject needs. Kohut was also aware that some patients responded negatively despite careful attempts on his part to be attuned. These patients were understood to have special difficulties in forming an empathic selfobject bond as a result of pervasive childhood deprivations which had left them in a continuous state of frustration and rage.

From a self psychological viewpoint, therefore, the drive manifestations of destructive rage are always moti-

vated by an injury to the self, and are considered to be
secondary breakdown products as a result of the disruption
in the empathic self-selfobject bond. Kohut was clear that
assertiveness and what can be described as constructive competitive aggressiveness are genuine and healthy human responses,
which he considered neither biologically drive-based nor secondary breakdown products of a self-selfobject disruption.

He makes a distinction between the competitive aggressiveness that occurs when someone or something stands in the way
of our achieving a goal, and the rage reactions which occur as a
result of traumatic deprivations by selfobjects. In the former, the
aggression which is directed to the interfering competing person
diminishes or ceases as soon as the goal is reached. This form of
aggressiveness, when it occurs in childhood, does not become the
nucleus of psychoneuroses (Kohut 1984, pp. 137–138). On the
other hand, narcissistic rage cannot be satisfied by an action
against the offender even when that action is effective, because
the damage to the self leads to a lingering hurt and rage. The
following vignettes illustrate this distinction.

Mr. X., who came to treatment because of complaints of marital
discord, felt that his relationship with his wife had been a tumultuous
one since they first met some fifteen years previously. Early in the
treatment he exemplified their difficulties by describing an incident in
which his wife had arbitrarily selected a decorative scheme for their
home without consulting him. This was particularly enraging to Mr.
X. since he had what he felt was a very creative plan of his own, which
had gone unrecognized and disregarded as evidenced by his wife's
unilateral decision. Though he was ultimately able to confront his
wife and have his viewpoints integrated into their plans, he continued
to feel enraged toward her about having been excluded in this way. As
treatment progressed he gradually was able to realize that his sensitivity to his wife's disregard was triggered by traumatic and deperso-
nalizing experiences he had had as a child when his thoughts and ideas

were given almost no validation or recognition. Therefore, his wife's overlooking his suggestions left him feeling very much as he had as a young boy. As a result of that serious childhood damage to his self, Mr. X's. destructive rage thus continued to simmer even after his ideas were acknowledged and integrated into the final decorating plan.

Mr. Q., who had come to treatment because of a vague sense of discontent with his life, became quite upset and angry that his employer had arbitrarily switched an appointment date without ever consulting him. Though his anger was intense he wasted little time in expressing his lack of appreciation of his employer's oversight. When the appointment was once again changed with the approval of Mr. Q., his anger subsided and the oversight was no longer an issue. Unlike Mr. X., Mr. Q. felt positive about himself for his success in correcting the oversight.

CHAPTER 8

Defense and Resistance

Classical psychoanalysis as well as the more contemporary psychoanalytic theories place a heavy emphasis upon the understanding and analysis of defense, or "resistance analysis." As Kohut worked from within the empathic stance of self psychology, he began to question whether this traditional conceptualization of resistance analysis held the same importance and meaning for self psychology.

CLASSICAL PERSPECTIVE

The conceptualizations of traditional psychoanalysis with regard to defense and to resistance analysis are based upon the
premise that the conscious mind – or, in later structural terms, the
ego and superego – defends or resists the emergence into consciousness of forbidden wishes, thoughts, and impulses. Consequently, the attitude of the psychoanalyst holding to these assumptions tends to be that of an objective scientist who views
the unconscious mind as an infected organ that needs to be lanced
and drained. In this analogy, the tissue covering the infection is
likened to the defenses that hold in check the instinctual wishes
that ultimately must be penetrated if the process of healing is to
take place. Though this analogy does not take into account the
many traditional analysts who sensitively utilize an empathic
approach in their interpretation of resistance, it does reflect a
general clinical attitude directly related to defense and resistance
theory.

In his early writings, Freud depicted an ideal psychoanalyst
as one who maintains the attitude of a ". . . surgeon, who puts
aside all his feelings, even his human sympathy . . ." (Freud
1912, p. 115) in order to penetrate the defenses to the infected
organ of the unconscious mind. Thus, resistance analysis represents a first step in gaining access to the drives, a goal which has
represented a therapeutic end-station in the psychoanalytic process. Once this process has been accomplished, the clinical theory
of traditional psychoanalysis suggests that all else will be accomplished – conflict resolution and analytic cure.

SELF PSYCHOLOGICAL PERSPECTIVE

Kohut acknowledged that the traditional model of defense and
resistance does explain delimited units of psychic function such

as slips of the tongue and other manifestations of psychopathology in everyday life. The traditional model also explains
aspects of psychic function in a majority of dreams (Kohut 1984,
p. 113). Where he found the model inadequate, however, was in
its explanation of personality in general and personality disturbances in particular.

How then does Kohut view defense and resistance within
the theoretical framework of self psychology?

First, Kohut thought that resistance is manifested in the
general reluctance of an individual to be in a narcissistically
vulnerable position vis-à-vis another person, such as in the patient–analyst dyad. This resistance is frequently seen in the
initial phase of a treatment – when a patient's inhibitions against
the formation of an empathic bond are strongest.

Second, Kohut thought that resistances were also manifested at certain important junctures during the course of a
treatment, particularly when some significant advance threatens
the equilibrium of the self. In general, therefore, Kohut preferred
to speak of a person's defensiveness rather than resistance. **He
understood the motivation for defensiveness as a need to
protect and preserve the cohesiveness of the self which in
some way is threatened.** This view of defense is, of course,
different from the traditional view that sees defense as the
dynamic forces of the ego warring against the emergence into
consciousness of discrete sexual and/or aggressive impulses.

Obviously the major difference in Kohut's understanding of
resistance as opposed to the traditional view is that, for Kohut,
resistance is an expression of creative psychological adaptation
that has allowed the individual to cope with less than optimal
early environmental circumstances. From this perspective the
implications for treatment are obvious. Defenses and resistances
are not seen as obstacles that need to be tolerated until eventually
broken down. Rather, the experience-near empathic stance per-

mits the analyst to understand the particular adaptive ability that the patient has developed. This understanding is part of the overall treatment process which promotes the transmuting internalization functions of the analyst and the unfolding of the selfobject transferences.

[For example] Ms. J., a 28-year-old single woman who had been in a previous psychoanalytic psychotherapy for approximately three years, terminated that treatment and after several months began treatment with a colleague of one of the authors.

Her initial complaint was an inability to form a satisfying relationship with a man. It seemed that all her relationships had ended within two or three years and left her feeling victimized, rejected, and angry, as the man had usually initiated the breakup. In her previous treatment her therapist had emphasized the masochistic nature of her behavior. He thought that in various ways she allowed the men she dated to hurt her emotionally. Her masochistic behavior was seen as punishment for the unconscious guilt of desiring to move emotionally away from her mother. Though interpretations in her previous therapy were directed to "separation–individuation" issues, the nature of her relationships remained basically the same. She continued to be mistreated, taken for granted, and ultimately rejected.

When she entered self psychological treatment, she possessed the same attitude with regard to the meaning of her behavior as did her previous analyst. She continually berated herself for her "masochism" and would frequently become enraged at herself for allowing people to take advantage of her. At the same time, she complained that she could not help herself. However, at times during the treatment she was able to express some feeling of pride in her ability to be sensitive to and thoughtful of others, even though she kept finding herself "being shortchanged." She appeared surprised when her analyst mirrored her recognition of her ability to be sensitive to others. Her immediate response was to dismiss the analyst's response with the comment, "Yes, but it is so masochistic." In time, she came to appreciate how much the investment in her self was tied to giving to others; she realized the extent to which she prided herself in "being there for others." She recalled that throughout her childhood she had been able to get some appreciation from her alcoholic mother, whom she took care of. When her mother was drunk, Ms. J. had assumed the responsibilities for maintaining the household. She came to understand how valuable her adaptive behavior had been in helping her to get some nurturance and validation for the preservation of her nuclear self vis-à-vis her generally abusive and intolerant mother.

As treatment progressed, Ms. J. came to understand that her way of giving to others was a means of feeling secure, accepted, and connected to these others. Rather than punishing herself, as the traditional view would interpret her behavior, Ms. J. was attempting to provide sustenance to her enfeebled self in the same way that had been available to her during her development.

This understanding led to the unfolding of the selfobject transferences, and to the movement away from her prototypical caretaking bond. As previously thwarted selfobject needs emerged, Ms. J.'s selfobject requirements and demands also underwent development. Her wish to serve others subsided. She now required her male friends to recognize her in a more equal way.

It can be pointed out here that the experience-near empathic stance in understanding human behavior has also led to a new understanding of those patients who, in traditional theoretical terms, would be considered to have defective defenses. The treatment of Mr. V. described in Chapter 16 illustrates this point.

CHAPTER 9

Dreams

Kohut (1977, pp. 108-111) postulates two types of dreams: (1) dreams that express underlying latent content (disguised wishes and conflict resolution) and (2) "self-state" dreams, which are dreams that attempt to bind nonverbal tensions of traumatic states, and, unlike the first type, are presented in an undisguised form.

DREAMS WITH LATENT CONTENT

In the first type, understanding the unconscious meaning of the dream (latent meaning) comes about through the patient's associations to the manifest content. Traditional as well as self psychologically informed analysts focus on understanding the meaning of the dream through the patient's associations. The understandings derived from these associations by the two types of analysis, however, may be quite different.

This difference in understanding is clearly illustrated in Kohut's "The Two Analyses of Mr. Z." (1979), in which Kohut gives his analyses of Mr. Z.'s dream of his father returning to the home first from a traditional and later from a self psychological perspective. The differences in understanding this dream are highlighted in Chapter 11.

An example of the first type of dream is one reported by the following patient in the middle phase of his treatment.

Mr. W., a 40-year-old married man and father of a 5-year-old son, initially entered treatment with complaints of depression and boredom in his work as a financial consultant. Much of the focus of the initial years of treatment was on his fear and resentment of male authority figures.

At around 4 years of age Mr. W. had suffered repeated disillusionment with his oedipal selfobject father, who rejected attempts by his son to idealize him. As a result of this deprivation, Mr. W. had become fixated on an early oedipal form of idealized parent imago. During his adult life he continually searched for powerful male figures to whom he would become attached, first idealizing them and then easily becoming disillusioned. With this as a background, Mr. W. reported the following dream during an important phase of his treatment:

> I was observing my son, who was standing at a train station, waiting for my father to arrive. He was so excited that he could hardly stand still. What struck me was that his face was bruised, and his heart was throbbing so hard I saw it make a bulge in his chest. When my father came he walked past my son and suddenly disappeared. I sensed some hurt on my son's face and I began crying in the dream. I woke up crying.

Mr. W. thought that his dream was triggered by his reading to his son on the night of the dream. While he was reading, he had been aware of his son's delight and enjoyment in this father–son activity. He added, "That enjoyment was something my father and I never had."

Associating to the dream, Mr. W. thought that his son's excitement followed by disappointment represented the many experiences he had had with his father as a child. He remembered how, on his eighth birthday, he had been looking forward to a particular toy gun which was promised to him. He remembered being given a wrapped gift and immediately knowing it was not the toy he wanted. His hopes were shattered and he wanted to cry. His father reprimanded him and threatened to punish him.

Mr. W. associated to the bruises on his son's face in the dream as representing his continuous disappointment and feelings of humiliation. In actuality his father had on occasion slapped him on the face.

Mr. W. associated to the throbbing and protruding of his son's heart from his chest as representing both the excitement in anticipating his idealized father's affection and the "heartbreak" which was his disappointment. His remembered reaction to the wrong present was also symbolic of his disappointment when he was unable to have the idealized, longed-for masculine strength (the powerful phallus, symbolized by the toy gun) of which he was deprived by his father's lack of confirming and validating affectionate responses.

While this is only a limited description of the full analysis of Mr. W.'s dream, it illustrates how self psychology has made possible an experience-near understanding of latent dream material. It can be pointed out here that viewing Mr. W.'s dream from an experience-distant vantage point would have led to a very different understanding as will be seen with Mr. Z.'s dream in Chapter 11.

SELF-STATE DREAMS

As already defined, self-state dreams are dreams that attempt to bind nonverbal tension of traumatic states because of the dreamer's dread of overstimulation or disintegration of the self through verbalizable imagery. Associations to the imagery in self-state dreams do not lead to the uncovering of latent content much like that of the dreams of children, or of those who have suffered severe traumatic situations or physical illness (Kohut 1977). The self-state dream in general expresses a disturbing change in the condition of the self such as a drop in self-esteem, overstimulation, or threat of the breakdown of the self.

Kohut suggests that interpretations of self-state dreams be made from the analyst's general knowledge of the patient's vulnerabilities, together with the specific situations that exacerbated those vulnerabilities and which brought about the disturbing change in the condition of the self.

Kohut offers an example of a self-state dream in the second analysis of Mr. Z. (1979). The dream occurred during that period of his analysis when he became aware of the positive qualities of his idealized selfobject father. The brief dream consisted of a starkly outlined image of his mother who was standing with her back turned toward him. Mr. Z. then experienced the most intense anxiety he had ever felt.

This self-state dream was an attempt by Mr. Z. to bind the threatening anxiety precipitated by his having relinquished the archaic selfobject connection with his mother. The dream imagery depicted his mother turning her back on him as a result of Mr. Z.'s developmental move away from her and toward the appreciation of the positive qualities and attributes of his father. The unseen side of his mother stood for her distorted personality and outlook which he had been forbidden to recognize. The dream also expressed his anxiety that his earlier conviction of his mother's power and superiority over his father, which had been so vital to his self-preservation, was, in fact, a delusion.

CHAPTER 10

The Curative Process

As we have pointed out repeatedly, Kohut underscores his belief that the empathic process is the means by which one can gain access into the inner life of another person for the purpose of understanding complex mental states. It is this empathic process that allows the treatment to move forward in what Kohut describes as a three-step movement, which includes analysis of the patient's defenses, unfolding of the selfobject transferences, and making possible the establishment of empathic intuneness between the self and its selfobjects on a mature adult level (Kohut 1984, pp. 65–66). In other words, the

111

self – which has been previously split off, repressed, and restricted to early archaic selfobjects – can now develop an empathic relatedness with a variety of new, enriching, and growth-producing selfobjects throughout life. Thus the healthy self is never viewed as separate and apart from its sustaining selfobjects.

The movement of the self from archaic to more mature selfobject ties is accomplished in the treatment process via the two basic steps of understanding and explaining. In self psychology, both of these phases of treatment take place within the context of the empathic process.

As we have pointed out, during the understanding phase the analyst attempts to grasp the experience of the patient and, in one form or another, attempts to communicate this understanding. With seriously disturbed patients, the understanding phase may require prolonged periods of immersion by the analyst.

In the explaining phase of treatment the analyst utilizes that understanding to eventually arrive at an in-depth genetic, dynamic, and economic interpretation. Of course the depth or level of explaining (interpretation) is determined by the level of the analyst's understanding and the readiness of the patient to accept a communication. This readiness is specifically discussed in the treatment of Ms. O. and Mr. V. in Part III of this book.

Kohut identifies an essential difference between understanding and explaining. He suggests that there is a decrease in the emotional intensity of the selfobject bond as the analyst moves from understanding to explaining. Nevertheless, whereas the intensity of the selfobject bond may be lessened as the patient becomes more objective about his self, the analyst's reconstructive explanation can deepen the selfobject connection on a more mature level as the patient gains deeper understanding and progresses in his or her development. Therefore, in the shift from understanding to explaining, the patient can continue to feel accepted by the selfobject analyst, even though what is communicated is increasingly more in-depth and objective.

Kohut compares this empathic shift from understanding to explaining in the treatment to the shift that occurs in a child's development from a bodily close form of empathy to one in which there is barely any touching. For example, the selfobject mother who may respond empathically to her infant's expressions of intense emotion with a warm and loving embrace, may respond just as appropriately many years later to similar affective states with a word, a glance, or a gesture. Thus the advance in the treatment process from understanding to explaining is analogous to the physical distance that gradually occurs in human development between the self and its selfobjects; at the same time, the empathic closeness is maintained.

CURE IN OTHER PSYCHOANALYTIC PERSPECTIVES

Kohut acknowledges the curative effects of other theoretical perspectives and believes that these positive results can be explained within the framework of self psychology. By this Kohut is not suggesting that all theory is just the same, and that therefore it does not matter what theory one holds. Self psychological theories are formulations derived from data collected from an experience-near vantage point, and therefore more accurately explain complex mental states. At the same time, Kohut does not deny the curative effects of other theoretical approaches.

How does self psychology account for the positive changes and successes that take place within other theoretical frameworks?

Kohut (1984, pp. 92-94) answers this question by citing

an example of a Kleinian analyst, who had announced during an
ongoing analysis that she would have to cancel a future session.
In the following session, the patient was withdrawn and silent.
Finally, after trying unsuccessfully to elicit some understanding
of this sudden mood shift, the analyst interpreted in a recogniz-
ably warm and understanding tone of voice that her cancellation
of a session had noticeably shifted the patient's view of her. She
further interpreted, in accord with Kleinian theory, that previously she had been the warm and supportive "good breast" but
had now become the depriving "bad breast." The analyst went
on to suggest that the patient's silence was her way of defending
against oral rage and the wish to tear apart the analyst as a bad
breast. To Kohut's surprise, this interpretation was effective
because, subsequently, the patient spoke openly and admitted
that since the last session her jaw muscles had been tight. She did
have angry biting fantasies toward the analyst. The hour concluded with the patient feeling better and being on good terms
with the analyst.

In Kohut's view the effectiveness of the intervention was
the analyst's empathic grasp of the patient's experience and the
communication of her understanding of that experience. The
analyst had told the patient that she knew how deeply upset the
patient was about having one of her appointments cancelled. In
other words, it was not the content of the interpretation but the
essential grasping and communicating of the patient's experience
that made the Kleinian analyst's intervention so helpful.

Kohut believes that this understanding aspect of the empathic activity is essential. Without experience-near understanding, no matter how correct the particular content of an interpretation—even when it is grounded in the theories of self
psychology—the intervention will be neither effective nor curative.

Clinical Applications of Self Psychology

CHAPTER 11

Kohut's Two Analyses

of Mr. Z.

Part III deals with clinical applications of self psychology. In this chapter we begin with a synopsis of Kohut's well known case, *The Two Analyses of Mr. Z.* (1979). This case exemplifies an analysis carried out in two installments of four years apiece, with a five-year hiatus separating the two. The first analysis was conducted while Kohut still held firmly to a traditional analytic position; the second was carried out when he was formulating his ideas on narcissism during the middle to late sixties. Thus, this case interestingly demonstrates the differences in theoretical perspective that influenced Kohut's clinical approach and ultimately his analytic process.

THE FIRST ANALYSIS

Introduction

Mr. Z., a handsome, physically well-built man in his mid-twenties, was the only child of wealthy parents. When he first began his analysis he was living alone with his widowed mother, his father having died some four years earlier, and was attending graduate school. His presenting complaints, though vague and diffuse, focused on somatic symptoms, a feeling of isolation and loneliness, and a personal assessment that he was not achieving to his potential in school. What had motivated him to seek treatment, however, something Kohut would learn later, was the loss of a male friend whose regular companionship had allowed Mr. Z. to maintain a psychic equilibrium in his relationship with his intrusive and overly controlling mother. He complained of difficulties in his relationships with women, admitting that his primary source of sexual gratification was masturbation accompanied by masochistic fantasies of being subjugated to domineering and powerful women.

Infantile material regarding the unremembered period of his earliest years, surmised from the overall quality of Mr. Z.'s personality and from a review of family photos and home movies, suggested that Mr. Z. was a happy child during his first year and a half. From all appearances he seemed to have been the apple of his mother's eye and a pleasure to his father.

A significant childhood event took place when Mr. Z. was $3\frac{1}{2}$ years of age. His father left the family to live with a nurse who had cared for him while he was hospitalized for a prolonged illness. Though the father returned a year and a half later when his son was 5 years old, the parents' relationship never improved and remained strained up until a few months before the father's death.

Treatment

The theme of the first year of this analysis was the "regressive mother transference." Mr. Z.'s demanding insistence that he be understood, his protests of anger when he was not, and his depletion and depression with analytic separations, such as weekends and vacations, were seen by Kohut as reenactments of that early year and a half when Mr. Z. had his mother all to himself. These symptoms were interpreted as transferential expressions of an early narcissistic relationship with a "doting" mother (as Kohut understood narcissism at the time), when the total exclusiveness of her attention to him went undisturbed by sibling rivals. During this first year of analysis, Kohut consistently interpreted Mr. Z.'s demanding and angry behavior as his wanting to maintain the delusion of having achieved an "oedipal victory," but this interpretation was met with angry and defensive protests on the part of the patient.

Despite these protests, Kohut held firm to his convictions that Mr. Z.'s stance was a regression from the oedipal and afixation in the phallic narcissistic stage, where he could maintain the fantasy that he had his mother exclusively to himself and that his rivalrous and castrating father had never returned to the home. Masturbatory fantasies of domineering women with phalli corroborated this theoretical perspective. For according to his theory at the time, Kohut viewed these masochistic fantasies as expressions of Mr. Z.'s unconscious guilt for his wish to possess his mother; in addition, Kohut viewed them as Mr. Z.'s way of denying his castration fears.

A warm and idealized relationship that Mr. Z. had with a male counselor, which began during his first summer camp experience in preadolescence and continued over a two-and-a-half year period, eventually ending with an overtly erotic homosexual act, offered Kohut further evidence for this oedipal explanation. Kohut viewed the counselor's role, particularly since this was Mr. Z.'s first prolonged separation from his home, as a replacement for the mother, the phallic woman.

After a year and a half into the analysis, Mr. Z.'s outbursts and demands subsided. This convinced Kohut that his theoretical understanding and explanations were finally taking hold. Mr. Z., on the other hand, insisted that his calmed demeanor was due not so much to a change in himself but that it was a response to something Kohut had said. Kohut had prefaced one of his interpretations with the remark, "Of course it hurts when one is not given what one assumes to be one's due." Although Kohut saw this explanation of his changed behavior as Mr. Z.'s further denial of his unresolved oedipal, he let the issue pass. He felt the analysis was now proceeding smoothly – that his patient was finally giving up his narcissistic investment in his preoedipal mother – and did not want to disrupt the evolving process with further confrontations. Evidence for the correctness of this theoretical explanation was found in the treatment's clinical success, which was manifest in several symptomatic and behavioral changes. Mr. Z. reported that his masochistic fantasies had diminished and eventually disappeared during the latter half of the analysis. He showed some important behavioral changes in that he had moved out of his mother's house and was living on his own. Finally, he not only began dating and having brief sexual encounters with women of his own age and culture, but eventually formed a more lasting relationship with one woman with whom he was contemplating marriage when his analysis terminated.

Kohut theorized that these changes had come about as a result of Mr. Z.'s gradually giving up his narcissistic demands during the first year and a half of the analysis, inasmuch as they represented a clinging to a preoedipal mother and the forestalling of an oedipal confrontation with an absent father. Consequently, as Mr. Z.'s narcissistic demands lessened, his expectations became more realistic and his masculine assertiveness – with women, in his career, and with Kohut in the transference – surfaced.

A final corroboration for Kohut's clinical explanation came in a dream six months prior to termination. Mr. Z.'s associations pointed clearly toward the time the father returned to the family.

> He was in a house, at the inner side of a door which was a crack open. Outside was the father, loaded with gift-wrapped packages, wanting to enter. The patient was intensely frightened and attempted to close the door in order to keep the father out. [p. 8]

Kohut's interpretations stressed the young man's ambivalence toward his father (". . . loaded with gift wrapped packages . . ." [but] the patient ". . . tried to close the door. . . ."). With this dream, Kohut made his patient aware of his hostility toward his father as an oedipal rival, and his fear of retribution in the form of castration at the hands of the strong and powerful male; and, finally, of his tendency to retreat either to the preoedipal attachment to the mother or to a submissive and passive homosexual attitude toward the father.

Termination

As this first analysis drew toward a close, Kohut felt confident because all seemed to have fallen into place according to the precepts of classical Freudian psychoanalysis. The oedipal conflict had been confronted, with its formally unconscious ambivalence toward the oedipal father having been exposed. The normally expected resistances against these unconscious conflicts surfaced, with temporary regression to and exacerbations of preoedipal issues. Added together with the observed symptom-

124   Clinical Applications of Self Psychology

atic and behavioral improvements, all evidence pointed to a
theoretically right and technically correct analytic process.

In retrospect, however, Kohut was able to identify one
factor that raised serious doubts about the validity of the changes
in the patient as well as the correctness of his theoretical explanations; namely, a shallowness and emptiness in Mr. Z.'s response to the termination phase of the treatment. Except for the
sadness connected with the loss of the analyst, this phase seemed
to lack the same zest and enthusiasm that was characteristic of
Mr. Z.'s response to other life situations, and that had been
prevalent during the earlier phase of this first analysis when Mr.
Z. had spoken lovingly and longingly about the preoedipal
mother or the admired camp counselor. Yet the analysis concluded with an expression of gratitude on Mr. Z.'s part and of
good wishes for the future on Kohut's.

THE PERIOD BETWEEN THE TWO ANALYSES

Three weeks after the termination of the analysis Mr. Z. sent a
brief letter to Kohut with his final payment. He stated that,
although he was finding that the loss of the analytic relationship
required an emotional adjustment, he felt he was doing "all
right." He also mentioned that he had decided not to marry but to
continue dating other women. There were two chance meetings
during this five-year period of time. Kohut surmised during brief
conversations at these times that Mr. Z. was not overly enthu-
siastic about his life, yet did not seem to be depressed.

THE SECOND ANALYSIS

Preliminary Consultations

Kohut was surprised when some four and a half years later Mr.
Z. wrote that he was again experiencing difficulties and that he

wished to return. Two preliminary consultations were had by
Mr. Z. prior to the actual start of the second analysis. In an initial
consultation six months before the treatment began, Mr. Z. gave
the impression of being under some emotional strain. Though he
spoke freely in the session, he indicated that little had changed in
his life since the end of the analysis. He was still living alone in
his own apartment. He was seeing no one particular woman,
and was becoming increasingly aware that his relationships with
women were empty and shallow. He also felt that his sex life
was unsatisfying. He mentioned in quick succession that there
had been no return of the addictive masturbation with masochistic fantasies, and that he found his work a burden and a chore.
Kohut surmised from the close connection of these two state-
ments – something that would be corroborated later, in the
second analysis – that the masochism evidenced in Mr. Z.'s earlier sexual fantasies had not been resolved, as Kohut had thought,
but had only been suppressed and displaced onto work and life in
general. Mr. Z. added that after a recent breakup with a girlfriend
he had become alarmed by a sense of isolation and a strong urge
to resort to his old addiction, compulsive masturbation with
masochistic fantasies.

A significant factor in Mr. Z.'s return to analysis had to do
with the emotional deterioration of his mother. Since his moving
from her home during the course of the first analysis, she had
become increasingly more isolated and paranoid. Kohut wondered if this worsening condition in the mother was not causally
connected to Mr. Z.'s own worsening condition. It was learned
later, to the surprise of both, that this occurrence was more a
positive motivator than an insidious deterrent to Mr. Z.'s health
and growth.

After a second consultation, it was agreed the analysis
would continue again in six months. Kohut was initially concerned about his patient's ability to wait that long, but was
reassured by Mr. Z.'s ready acceptance of the postponement of

treatment and by his comment that he had been feeling better since the first consultation. Kohut indeed recognized this difference in him. In the second consultation Mr. Z. held himself more erectly, moved with more bounce, and spoke more confidently. Based on this significant shift in his patient's mood and demeanor, Kohut hypothesized the emergence of an idealized selfobject transference. This initial hypothesis found confirmation in a dream that occurred on the night before the first session of the second analysis. The dream contained no story and no action, but was simply the image of a man who was "strong and confidence-inspiring." Associations pointed to the figure as representing Kohut, the camp counselor, and the patient's father. The idealizing nature of the transference was suggested both by the "proud bearing" of the figure, and by the tone of admiration with which Mr. Z. spoke about the man. An association to the earlier "father" dream of the first analysis highlighted for Kohut the fact that this analysis was a continuation of the first, and was picking up at the point where the first had failed most significantly.

After approximately two weeks this initial idealization subsided and was replaced by a secondary mirror transference of a merger type. Thus, from a state of calmness and buoyancy he fell back into the demanding self-centeredness that had typified the initial phase of the first treatment.

Kohut assumed a quite different attitude toward this phase of the analysis than he had in the first treatment. Whereas then Mr. Z.'s wish for empathic attunement was judged to be an unreasonable demand and viewed as a need to control Kohut, in the second analysis this same behavior was looked upon within the transference as a ". . . valuable replica of a childhood condition that was being revived in the analysis" (p. 12). Mr. Z.'s demand for empathic mirroring was taken seriously and was recognized as an important need; this attitude on Kohut's part lessened the patient's iatrogenically induced rage and brought new understandings to formerly unexplored sectors of his personality.

The focus of the analysis now centered upon the personality of the mother, who had previously been perceived as responding to Mr. Z. with enjoyment and as a doting parent whose love for her son remained unquestioned. In the second analysis, Mr. Z. reexamined their relationship. In time he was able to acknowledge that his mother's love and acceptance were not totally unconditional. He came to realize, in fact, that his mother's caring was at the cost to him of submitting to her will, which involved the inhibition of his autonomous urges and the exclusion of any independent relationship aside from the one he had with her. Though he now knew that he had preconsciously experienced his father's departure from the home as an abandonment of him, Mr. Z. could now appreciate his father's wish to escape from Mr. Z.'s jealous and possessive mother. In his second analysis, feeling greater support from Kohut because of his changed attitude and perspective, Mr. Z. could now acknowledge the bizarreness of certain behaviors of the mother (the ritualistic removal of blackheads from his face during his childhood as well as the inspection of stools) that formerly he had seen as expressions of her loving attention toward him. Even in normal everyday interactions such as the mother's reading to the son, playing with him and sharing stories about his future pursuits, there was an unstated and clear assumption that he would never leave her and would remain with her as a permanent selfobject. In time Kohut acknowledged the borderline nature of the mother's personality and of the essential mirroring function served by her son for the maintenance of her own self-cohesion. This had enabled her to ward off a confrontation with an underlying psychotic core, which finally manifested itself in her paranoid delusions when Mr. Z. moved out of the house and into his own apartment.

Recognizing the rigidity of the mother's pathological per-

sonality, and considering Mr. Z.'s previously unanalyzed charac-
terological response of submissiveness and compliance, enabled
Kohut to understand Mr. Z.'s lack of genuine personality change
in the first analysis and the shallowness of the previous termination phase. Kohut also understood that his own allegiance to his
classical theories had become for Mr. Z. a replica of his mother's
distorted outlook on the world, which he had accepted. Mr. Z.
had submitted to Kohut's convictions similarly to the way he
had submitted to his mother's. For example, he had acceded to
Kohut's oedipal interpretations, suppressing his masturbatory
urges and displacing his masochistic fantasies onto work and life
in general. In short, Kohut recognized that Mr. Z.'s changes had
not been permanent because they were due to a transference
success.

In the second analysis, the issue of Mr. Z.'s compliance
became a primary focus. With each step in the process of sorting
out which reality was correct – that which he had learned in the
first analysis, that which his mother had taught him, or that
which he was now coming to in the second analysis – Mr. Z.
experienced periods of intense fear and resistance followed by
feelings of exhilaration as he found his self becoming steadily
disentangled from the merger enmeshment with his selfobject
mother. It was within this context that Mr. Z.'s joy over his
initial recognition of his mother's mental illness, very puzzling to
him at first, was understood.

Reconsideration was given, in light of these new understandings, to Mr. Z.'s childhood sexual activities, such as his
compulsive masturbation and his primal scene activities.
Whereas they had been viewed in the first analysis as infantile
modes of pleasure gain through drive gratification, those activities were now seen as a source of stimulation for the young boy's
empty and incapacitated self. The normal stimulation that might
have been provided by the gradual movement toward indepen-

dence, autonomy, and self-delimitation was denied to Mr. Z. because of his total submission to his domineering mother; stimulation was therefore sought in the addictive sexual activities of his childhood and even his adulthood. His masochistic tendencies were interpreted not so much as expressions of unconscious guilt for sexually desiring the oedipally forbidden mother and "killing off" the castrating father, but as the unconscious enmeshment with the rigid and dominant mother.

The second half of the second analysis was marked by opening a channel of empathy to the repressed idealized selfobject father. Initially, this new focus was marked by a receding of the depressive elements that were previously prominent, and the emergence of a new tone of vitality and hopefulness. Mr. Z. first spoke of the disappointment he had always felt toward his father for not standing up to the mother, as well as for his abandonment of him and leaving him to his mother.

Mr. Z. came to understand at this time that the loss of his longtime friend's companionship, which had brought him to treatment in the first place, had upset him in a similar way as had his father's departure many years earlier. In other words, without the idealized father's presence he had been unable to become disentangled from the merger enmeshment with the selfobject mother. At the same time, his preadolescent involvement with the camp counselor, which had originally been understood as a displaced fixation upon the preoedipal mother, was now interpreted as an expression of Mr. Z.'s seeking out of ". . . the yearned-for figure of a strong fatherly man . . ." (p. 19).

A major turning point in the second analysis took place in a second phase of Mr. Z.'s "move toward the father." In a mood of exhilaration, Mr. Z. began to recollect positive qualities and strengths of his father he had previously not recognized. These recollections were accompanied by severe anxieties, even psychotic-like states, which Kohut now understood as the patient's psychic shift from an archaic attachment to his selfobject mother to the emergence of a "nuclear self" linked to the formerly repressed, idealizing selfobject image of the strong father.

During this period a dream of the mother with her back to her son caused Mr. Z. the greatest anxiety he had ever experienced. It came to be understood in its most obvious content as the mother's icy withdrawal from her son as he now moved toward independence. The faceless nature of the mother's image was understood as representing her ". . . distorted personality and her pathological outlook on the world and on him . . ." (p. 20).

Memories of a ski trip taken with his father when Mr. Z. was only 9 years old highlighted strong qualities that made the father's personality admirable. Rather than feeling defeated by these fatherly strengths, as the classical oedipal view would expect him to be, the patient now felt invigorated by his growing awareness that he had an image of masculine strength with which he could merge while consolidating his own independent and autonomous masculine self.

Termination

The termination phase of the second analysis began with a return to the dream that had marked the conclusion of the first analysis—namely, the dream in which Mr. Z. was closing the door to prevent his gift-bearing father from coming into the house. As a result of the new understanding gained in this second analysis, and through Mr. Z.'s associations, the dream was no longer seen as referring to his hostility toward his father and his fear of castration, and signifying a retreat to the preoedipal position with his mother. Rather, the dream was seen to depict the fright that Mr. Z. had experienced at the sudden return of his father to the home. Whereas Mr. Z. had longed for his father and his psychological "gifts," his self development at that point disallowed him from taking in and internalizing the yearned-for male image by suddenly moving away from the sustaining selfobject bond with the mother and moving instead toward the returning father.

At this point in the treatment, Mr. Z. began to experience himself in two separate ways – one as a slave bonded to his powerful and domineering mother, and the other as a potentially strong and independent male firmed by the merger with the idealized image of his father. The one sector contained the grandiosity of his being admired by his selfobject mother as long as he remained faithful to her demands (vertical split); the other contained the disavowal of his bond to the idealized selfobject father (horizontal split). Kohut recognized only two periods in Mr. Z.'s life which allowed for an opening to this disavowed sector: the earlier relationship with the camp counselor, and the idealizing selfobject transference of this second analysis. The slow but steady working-through process of the latter led to a successful termination, in which Mr. Z. could depart the analytic relationship unencumbered by the previous burdens of his masochistic attachment to his selfobject mother, and buoyant with feelings of autonomy, independence, and joy. Later it was learned that Mr. Z. had married a well-balanced and warm-hearted woman, and that he had reached such a level of success in his career that he was regarded as outstanding in his field.

CHAPTER 12

Treatment of a Narcissistic Personality Disorder: The Case of Ms. O.

The following case illustrates the treatment of a woman (Ms. O.) who was considered to have a narcissistic personality disorder. As stated earlier, Kohut (1977) defined this disorder as a temporary breakup, enfeeblement, or distortion of the self. This disorder is one of the two primary self disturbances. The second is the narcissistic behavior disorder in which symptoms are manifested in behavior such as perversion, addiction, or delinquency.

As previously discussed in Chapter 6, Kohut (1984) broadly differentiated the narcissistic personality and behavior disturbances from the psychoses and borderline states in terms of the degree of establishment of a nuclear self. Unlike the psychoses, and also unlike the borderline states – which Kohut has defined as covert psychotic personalities but with developed defensive structures – narcissistic disturbances have a more structured development of a basic nuclear self that can be strengthened.

We hope to illustrate how the use of self psychology has contributed to the understanding and the treatment of Ms. O. The initial session, another session in the seventh month of treatment, and one in the sixteenth month will be highlighted as an integral part of the overall discussion of the treatment. In the presentation of the sessions the analyst has attempted to reveal his ongoing thoughts and reactions as accurately as possible so that the reader can take part in the session as it proceeds from moment to moment. Also, throughout these sessions and the summary of the treatment, the theory of self psychology will be explicated so that the reader can gain a theoretical understanding of the treatment process. The analyst's thinking, which includes both his moment-to-moment reactions and theoretical understanding, will follow specific segments of the sessions. We are aware that this format may make it more difficult for the reader to follow the patient–analyst dialogue than if there were no interruptions. However, we think that the moment-to-moment considerations provide the reader with an opportunity to fully explore and understand the nuances of the treatment as it occurred.

EXPANDING ATTUNEMENT

We have also attempted to demonstrate a mode of empathic listening which we have defined as "expanding attunement" to what the patient is experiencing. It requires continuous empathic immersion into the patient's shifting states of thinking and feeling. This is not only a matter of hearing the content of what the patient says, but is also an attunement to *how* the patient experiences what he or she says (Basch 1980). Therefore, the meaning of the patient's thoughts, ideas, fantasies, and so on is derived not only from the verbalized content but from how the patient experiences what he or she says or thinks.

Expanding attunement is an intersubjective process whereby the analyst attempts as closely as possible to experience what the patient is experiencing, which includes the patient's simultaneous experience of the analyst. It is not just an attunement to a specific affective coloring of a particular thought, idea, or fantasy expressed at a given moment; rather, it retains the cumulative moments of the patient's experience that the analyst has perceived and that continually widen and deepen the analyst's understanding. In this sense expanding attunement is the analyst's emotional canvas of the patient's shifting, changing, and widening experiences, which continually add new details to a slowly developing portrait.

Whether or not the analyst's perception of the patient's unfolding experience approximates that which the patient is experiencing is determined by the patient's continuous responses to the analyst's communications. If the patient feels understood, it can be assumed that the analyst's perception is at least generally correct. There are exceptions, however. Severely disturbed patients may sometimes respond negatively to a closely attuned empathic communication. This issue is highlighted later in our discussion of the treatment of Mr. V.

THE TREATMENT

The following describes the treatment of Ms. O., a 26-year-old Hispanic woman who suffered a number of self disturbances.*

---

*The interchanges presented here were taken from notes that were written after the sessions.

She was considered to have a narcissistic personality disorder because, on a symptomatic level, she experienced temporary feelings of loss of self which were manifested by hypersensitivity to comments by friends, feelings of worthlessness, depression, and a number of bodily pains which seemed to come and go according to her level of anxiety. There was no history of adapting to difficulties through various forms of behavior, which is, as previously stated, the distinguishing factor which differentiates the narcissistic personality disorder from the narcissistic behavior disorder.

My initial impression of Ms. O. as suffering from a narcissistic disorder was substantiated later in the treatment as she developed a stable selfobject transference.

Referral Information

I knew only that Ms. O. was a young woman, 26 years of age, married, and highly anxious. The referral person said that this Hispanic woman was suffering from a number of physical symptoms – headaches, sore throat, back and leg pains.

Initial Interview

Ms. O. entered my office as if she were in a rush. She passed by me quickly with her head down and eyes lowered. Her face was flushed and I had the distinct feeling that she was embarrassed.

Here, I attempted to immerse myself into her experience. It should be pointed out that focusing on the patient's experience (experience-near) is different from responding to the person per se (experience-distant). If I had made no attempt to capture what she was experiencing, I might have focused on a number of personal feelings about such things, for example, as the way she seemed to ignore my presence and her rushing by me. Whereas it can be argued within certain theoretical circles that personal responses to the patient are valuable diagnostic tools, self psychology maintains that it is through the *patient's experience* that we can truly understand the psychological meaning of his or her behavior.

As I continued my efforts to capture her experience, I sensed that she was not only embarrassed but was afraid to look up at me. She quickly took a seat before I could offer her one. Her voice was weak and had a breathless quality to it.

Here, I am observing from an experience-distant perspective for the purpose of helping me capture her subjective feeling.

When she lifted her eyes, I sensed a prayerful quality about her as if she saw someone of great importance. She was petite and pretty. Her face was youthful and cherub-like. She wore no makeup. Her long black hair that flowed over her shoulders seemed to hide her body. As she sat motionless in her chair, I sensed the shyness of a "good little girl." Her gaze remained fixed on the floor except for an occasional furtive glimpse at me. I sensed her experiencing me as an important and powerful figure. At that moment, I was aware of beginning to feel important.

Here, I was aware of my own evoked response to my capturing her experience of me as important. Again, this is different from evoked reactions to the person of the patient – that is, from the experience-distant vantage point. I felt I could say anything and she would accept it. I felt admired and important, and I liked it. For a brief moment I let my fantasy run free and imagined myself as a wise and beneficent ruler dressed in a regal robe. I questioned whether or not I could use my fantasy to understand her experience. Was my experience of the moment close to hers? I soon learned that it was not. In fact, Ms. O.'s experience of me was not of my being a beneficent figure. Rather she experienced me as punitive and intolerant. The important point to be emphasized here is that the only way to discern accurately what the patient is experiencing is through empathic immersion.

Thus far I tentatively thought I might be observing some fleeting form of an idealizing transference.

Ms. O. began to cry. After some moments she began to speak almost inaudibly, "I'm glad to have someone to speak with since my husband wanted me to. He is concerned about my leg and back pains and feels there is something wrong–you know, maybe some nerve disease. Also, I have this cold in my chest–X-rays of my chest were O.K., but I don't believe it. All my medical tests were O.K. I don't believe that either. (She paused). I can tell you understand–I am glad I have an older man. My doctor first suggested someone else–a younger man–but I didn't want a young man. I don't know why– I don't think that I could depend on a younger man. I don't think that I could trust a woman either." Ms. O.'s voice seemed stronger.

She suddenly became silent. After some moments she anxiously said, "I don't know why I said that–I never talk about anyone. I am weak and a crybaby, not like my husband. When my husband goes on business trips, I am up the wall–the depression and emptiness are too much. I become a crazy woman–screaming–and all that."

Here, my immersion into Ms. O's experience made it possible for me to be attuned to the subtle shifts in her affective states from mild fearfulness to forcefulness and suddenly to intense anxiety. I thereby came to a very tentative understanding that she was allowing herself to risk a momentary movement away from what I provisionally began to consider as the nucleus of an idealizing selfobject transference, to an expression of assertiveness. My attunement also made it possible for me to sense Ms. O.'s subtle and immediate shift back to experiencing herself as anxiously helpless ("I'm weak and a crybaby") in comparison to her husband, whom she seemed to experience as idealized and superior. Whereas my understanding was necessarily provisional in these early moments of treatment, my empathic listening within the patient's experience afforded me at least hints of the quality, form, and intensity of Ms. O.'s thwarted selfobject needs. These early hints, like the sketchy outlines of a beginning painting, serve to identify areas of the patient's needs.

After some moments Ms. O. continued: "It is unfair that only he has trips to take and so many friends. Maybe he has other women. I want more friends – a lot more."

Once again, I sensed a moment of assertiveness as she complained about the unfairness in her relationships. I tentatively surmised that her assertiveness was evidence of an emerging grandiose self.

With considerable intensity, she said sharply, "This is crazy. I'm not a good enough wife. Why shouldn't he look at other women. I am the one who is sick. My husband is a fine man." She began to cry softly and then to sob. After some moments she became quiet and looked at the floor.

Here, I continued my effort to be in her experience, and, as much as possible, to widen my scope of attunement in order to follow her rapid emotional shifts. At this point I was able to come to a firmer initial understanding that Ms. O. was shifting from expressing grandiosity to experiencing herself as helpless. For example, once again, and with greater intensity, Ms. O. had inhibited her assertiveness ("This is crazy ") as she acknowledged complaints and desires ("I want more friends . . .").

I thought at this point that my initial understanding was firm enough in my mind to communicate, which would thereby facilitate the treatment process. However, the question can be asked here: How does the analyst know just how much of his or her understanding should be shared so that the patient can feel understood, especially in beginning communications? It can be suggested that the level of understanding that an analyst can effectively communicate is determined by his or her degree of empathic attunement to what the patient is experiencing, and by whether the patient has some awareness of his or her own experience. For example, Ms. O. was undergoing a painful struggle in her attempt to share her turmoil with me. It was this overall experience with which she seemed to be in touch (available to her preconscious and conscious mind). This available experience can be defined as the experience "in ascendancy." Communication outside of the patient's experience in ascendancy invariably results in the patient feeling misunderstood.

It was on Ms. O.'s painful experience of struggle, which I sensed was in ascendancy, that I focused my intervention.

I said: "I am aware that it is not an easy task to let me in on these painful thoughts and feelings."

My communication was directed to her emerging assertiveness ("... when you were letting me in on your thoughts") and to her resistance ("... it is not an easy task ...").

She said, "That's right, I never thought I could say these things. I even feel better. The pains in my arm went away."

Ms. O.'s ability to recognize her strength was solid and lasted for some moments. The upbeat quality of her voice, the acknowledgment of her ability, and the generally positive tone of her response suggested that my communication was meaningful. This is the evidence that we use to determine the "accuracy" or "inaccuracy" of our interventions.

She said: "I know you are wise and must think that I am ungrateful and shameful. You must think I'm crazy. I want to apologize for this temper tantrum. I was like a child telling you crazy things. As my husband says, I am trying to manipulate you. Can't stand myself for my manipulation. Please don't listen to these baby ways of mine. Don't know if you will work with me if I go on this way."

Here, I experienced a quality of desperation in her that I had not been aware of before. She seemed frightened, and, like a fish out of water, plunged back into the safety position of idealizing through exalting me over herself ("I know you are wise . . . You must think I'm crazy ").

I viewed Ms. O.'s form of idealization as "primitive" in that she experienced herself as helpless, and subservient to an all-wise and powerful figure. It could be described as a slave-to-master selfobject bond. As discussed earlier, this suggests that there have been traumatic disappointments in the idealized parent and that fixations on an archaic form or forms of the idealized parental imago (image) have occurred.

Though this form of idealization was painful to her, I sensed that the acceptance of her assertiveness posed an even more formidable threat, as evidenced, for example, by her desperation. This suggested that Ms. O. had perhaps suffered even more severe traumas affecting the development of her exhibitionistic or grandiose self. It further suggests that fixations have occurred on primitive forms of the grandiose self configurations and with it stereotypical magical thoughts of power, destruction, and annihilation.

As treatment proceeds, it is important that the specifics of

the traumas be analyzed, insofar as they relate to the formation
of fixations on archaic forms of the grandiose self and on idealized parental imagoes, so that new editions of the self-selfobject
ties can be allowed to develop.

The total empathic process which includes the two steps of
treatment – understanding and explaining – facilitates the development of the selfobject transferences. The initial step offers the
essential confirming responses that allow the patient to feel
understood. This is the first step, but as indicated earlier it is by no
means the only one if a true analytic cure is to be accomplished.
The full empathic process, including various levels of explaining,
provides the patient with the awareness of the resistances against
emerging selfobject transferences, and allows for the working
through of inhibiting anxieties and the internalization of the
anxiety-relieving functions of the selfobject analyst. This in turn
further promotes the development of the selfobject transferences
as fixations are loosened and as compensatory structures are
formed.

As previously discussed, the concept of resistance in self
psychology is resistance to the development of the selfobject
transferences. Resistances have to do with the anticipated unempathic responses by the analyst. There also can be resistance to
empathy. In such cases the patient guards against trusting because of the severe narcissistic traumas that he or she suffered as
a child.

Resistance in self psychology involves the use of defensive
processes, defense mechanisms, and any other mental activities
that interfere with the analysis and, therefore, the development
of selfobject transferences.

I postulated that Ms. O.'s major trauma was in the exhibitionistic sector of her self as she seemed to be much less anxious
when she was in the pathological idealizing bond. My observation of Ms. O.'s ability to form self-selfobject ties in one or the

other sectors of the self was important in determining the areas of trauma as well as whether she had an "analyzable" self disorder. The understanding of the nuclear pathology is important not only in the ongoing treatment but in termination. For a successful termination, treatment must have dealt with exposing the primary defects of the self; it must also have made functionally reliable the formerly defective primary structures; and/or it must have made possible the development of reliable compensatory structures (Kohut 1977, p. 4).

As Ms. O. retreated from her assertiveness (exhibitionism), toward the primitive idealizing bond where she experienced herself as diminished, I sensed that her experience in ascendancy was that she was despicable. To make any clarification as to her shift in experiences seemed premature. In other words, I felt that she needed to experience this diminished position – not to analyze it. At this point, however, I thought in drive-conflict terms which indicated that she was punitively turning aggression on herself. It was with this in mind that I made the next intervention.

I said, "It seems you are being pretty hard on yourself."

As soon as I spoke I was immediately aware that I was bringing something in that was not in her experience.

She responded: "I don't know what you mean but I never know what people mean. You see I'm stupid, too. I'm a mess. I'm embarrassed. I've talked more than I have for months and that's what embarrasses me."

I realized that by being out of her experience I had severely interfered with the beginning development of the selfobject bond. My understanding and communication were not attuned to what she was experiencing. Ms. O. was embarrassed. She retreated further into the idealizing bond where she felt even more diminished. She explained my lack of attunement as her lack ("I never know what people mean"). In reflecting upon it, I realized that my intervention should have related only to her experience of feeling painfully diminished – not to the fact that she was producing it. However, Ms. O.'s ability to be assertive and to reveal painful events as well as to question them emerged again.

With more intensity than before, she said, "Why am I embarrassed? I hang around my husband like a puppy dog without a thought of my own. Was I always like this? I can't remember, but I do know that I've been rejected. Can you imagine what it's like to wait at home and wonder if he is going to come home and what woman is going to call and ask for him? He doesn't even want children." She paused. "Why am I complaining again? I don't complain. That's not like me. My husband is right. I am lucky to have a home and to be married. Many women can't find husbands." She began to cry. She wiped her eyes and then became quiet.

Here, Ms. O. allowed herself to be even more assertive before retreating to the idealizing bond. I was aware that throughout the session Ms. O. was sharing with me an increasingly wider range of painful affects and nuances of her thinking and experiencing, within both sectors of the self. As the session progressed, she voiced more complaints about her husband and her life situation even though her emerging grandiosity precipitated more intense levels of anxiety and deeper levels of regression to the diminishing idealizing bond. Unlike my first intervention, in which I related only to Ms. O.'s assertiveness, I sensed that now I could relate to her helplessness as well as her assertiveness, both of which seemed to be in ascendancy. However, I sensed that it was premature to share with her my understanding of the dynamics of the shifts, as I did not sense that she was in any way curious or interested in the "why" of what was going on.

I said, "You are letting me in on a number of painful feelings – the unfairness as well as the feelings of helplessness. I get the picture you are going through an awful lot." Ms. O. responded with a smile, "Yes, that is true. I am painting more and more of a picture. Maybe I should be a writer? People who are writers have had to go through a lot." She then became anxious and somewhat sad. "Guess that is stupid for me to say. I am not smart. I am no philosopher like my husband. Guess I should not be here – don't even think I can understand myself."

As in my first intervention, Ms. O. was able to accept my communication and give herself credit for her ability to express her painful thoughts ("People who are writers have had to go through a lot "). I was aware that the intensity of the diminishing idealizing bond was less.

Without a pause in her speaking, she quickly became assertive. There seemed to be less anxiety. The tone of her voice was unwavering and considerably stronger. "I don't know if that is true, I'm not so sure I am so different from all the other women my husband says are more cultured. He always compares me [to them] and says that is why he has to have many friends – that I could never really be on their level." (She experienced a pain in her back.) "There's my pain again. It's the first time I've noticed it starting. That's strange. Maybe it will go away – maybe you can take it away quickly and for good. It takes away all pleasure from life – this pain. I hope that you will see me."

I said, "I would like to work with you." Ms. O. paused. Her hands began to tremble. "Maybe I am too sick to do this," she said. "I don't want to waste your time. Other people would be able to use your time better."

Ms. O. went on to describe how she had felt as a little girl growing up in a Puerto Rican ghetto outside of San Juan. She remembered the poverty and crowded conditions in her house where she had slept with two sisters and three brothers in the same room. Throughout her description, I got the impression that she was retreating to the experience of herself as unworthy and beyond help. I also got the impression that she wished me to agree with her – again, I thought it to be one of those times when she needed to reinstate her prototypical idealizing bond.

I said, "It feels kind of useless to think about coming here?" She responded, "Yes, that's right." She began to sob. "You understand, don't you? I do want to try for awhile if that is all right with you?" I said, "Of course." At this point we arranged a time for another session, and I told her my fee.

My intervention, "It feels kind of useless to think about coming here?" was directed to her experience of feeling worthless and hopeless, which was in ascendancy. It related solely to her diminished position. Unlike my earlier intervention in which I did not stay with her conviction of worthlessness ("It seems you are being pretty hard on yourself "), I was able here to remain in her experience. Ms. O. felt understood and relieved. One could postulate here that her feeling understood permitted the further development of an idealizing selfobject transference ("You understand, don't you?"), which in turn permitted her to consider going on with the treatment.

CHAPTER 13

Expanding Attunement to the Patient's Shifting Experience: The Case of Ms. O.

In this initial session my emphasis was on continually expanding my attunement to Ms. O.'s shifting experiences, in order to get as full an initial understanding as possible within my own individual limitations for empathy. It goes without saying that as the scope of the therapist's sensitivity to the nuances of the patient's experiences increases over time, so does the completeness of the understanding which can then be provided to the patient. This sensitivity must encompass the patient's readiness for interpretations as well as the nature of the interpretations themselves. It should be emphasized that immersion into the patient's experience is not simply unidirectional as it is when one vicariously experiences a character in a movie or a play. Rather, experiencing the patient is an intersubjective process wherein the patient's experience is in some way continuously affected by the analyst. The analyst's experience of the patient's experience (experiencing you) is a fluid and constantly changing process with no moment the same as the one before. While this process may seem complicated in its description, the analyst can feel comforted in the fact that whatever the patient's experience, it can be determined by maintaining the experience-near position.

This intersubjective process as we have discussed it is not to be confused with what is commonly referred to as the "interpersonal" process between analyst and patient. The interpersonal process focuses on how the "person" (behavior, affects, and so on) of the analyst and patient mutually affect each other from an experience-distant perspective.

A CONTRAST TO THE STANDARD PSYCHIATRIC INTERVIEW

It could be said that Ms. O.'s initial interview failed in that I did not obtain enough specific information regarding the patient's past history or current functioning to get an adequate diagnostic impression, in order to determine the feasibility of treatment and goals and—more importantly—whether there is a potential for depression, suicide, addiction, or the like. Obtaining facts about the patient's life situation has been an important goal of the standard psychiatric interview, and is frequently required by insurance companies for third-party reimbursements as well as by mental health facilities for record-keeping purposes.

A satisfactory and just consideration of these important and complex issues would require lengthy deliberation, and goes beyond the scope of this work. However, at the risk of oversimplifying, I would like to briefly mention three issues which have led to the standard formulation of diagnostic profiles and setting of treatment goals. These are: (1) the therapist's belief in the theoretical validity of the standard approach in beginning treatment, (2) the therapist's interest in protecting against malpractice suits especially in the case of potentially suicidal patients, and (3) the investment by insurance companies and many mental health facilities in the goal of limiting the length of treatment and restricting the therapeutic process to the achievement of predetermined treatment goals.

Self psychology emphasizes that true psychological understanding of complex mental states is born out of experience-near data gathering. For example, through prolonged empathic immersion into the patient's experience, the analyst can determine with some accuracy the overall condition of the self – the degree of cohesiveness, areas of weakness and strength, reliance on defensive structure, propensity for the development of compensatory structure, levels of anxiety and depression, potential for constructive and self-destructive behavior, and prognosis. Self psychology's experience-near focus in gathering information is in contrast to the usual diagnostic first interview, in which the focus is on inquiry and questioning from an experience-distant vantage point. The experience-distant approach to questioning and inquiry is grounded in a body of theory which supports the belief that this form of objective inquiry is the most helpful way to obtain a picture of the patient's needs and pathology and thus determine the correct course of treatment.

It is reasoned that because this approach provides immediate access to many of the objective facts of the patient's life, the

analyst can be alerted to characteristic patterns of past functioning. This is especially important in satisfying those legal requirements to report incidents of past child abuse and patients who are
potentially homicidal or threatening, and in taking protective
measures against lawsuits in the case of potentially suicidal
patients.

How then can a self psychological approach in this initial
interview with Ms. O. be justified in light of the above issues?
Although I did not ask questions as to Ms. O.'s feelings of
helplessness and depression or whether there were feelings or
actual thoughts of suicide, I was able to come to a beginning
understanding of the depth of her despair through my empathic
immersion into what she was experiencing. I was able to achieve
the following: (1) I sensed her assertiveness and forcefulness,
which grew stronger throughout the session even in the face of
mounting anxiety and retreats to more intense feelings of helplessness, all of which she tolerated. (2) I sensed a hopefulness and
a desire to begin treatment and rid herself of pain. These as well
as other nuances helped me to formulate a beginning impression
of her areas of weakness and strength. (3) Her positive responses
to my interventions helped me to evaluate both her potential for
treatment and my ability to help her. (4) Finally, I came to a
general awareness of Ms. O.'s goals for herself. She wished to rid
herself of the pain and anxiety of feeling unequal to her husband,
and she wished to make more friends and in general expand her
activities.

INQUIRY AND QUESTIONS IN SELF PSYCHOLOGY

There is a major point that is illustrated by the initial session with
Ms. O. Whereas the sort of inquiry used in self psychology takes

an experience-near route, in contrast with the experience-distant approach of the usual psychiatric interview, both approaches enable diagnostic impressions to be formulated to meet administrative and insurance requirements. **Also, whereas self psychology objects to the "experience-distant" questioning or inquiry as failing to provide meaningful data from the patient's experience, it does not object to questions being asked – as long as the inquiry is within the patient's experience and ultimately serves the goals of the empathic process, which are understanding and explaining.** As with explaining, questioning the patient can be viewed as being more removed from the patient's experience than is understanding. However, as with explaining, the therapist's inquiry may serve to deepen the patient's feeling of being understood.

The following is an example of how the empathic "experience near" process led to an understanding of the depth of the patient's despair and to asking a specific question.

Ms. P., 61 years of age, was referred for consultation by her physician, Dr. X. She was seen to be in good physical health but depressed by her recent divorce. Her depression was exacerbated by the loss of her pet cat which had been run over by an automobile shortly after her divorce was finalized.

Ms. P. was late for her session and immediately began to apologize that she had lost track of the time. Focusing on her experience, I immediately sensed that Ms. P. was struggling against what seemed to be a heaviness in her walk and speech. It was almost as if she were trying to keep herself awake by her somewhat rapid speech and by motions which seemed strained and forced. As she sat down, she simultaneously slumped into the chair and for a brief second closed her eyes. Ms. P. was a petite, slim, neatly and fashionably dressed woman who seemed younger than her years. She again apologized for her lateness, then quickly said, "I don't know what to say to put some order into things."

I sensed that Ms. P. was speaking with great effort, but in a disinterested and mechanical way as if reciting a memorized speech. I further sensed that her struggle to speak was the experience in ascendancy. If so, perhaps Ms. P. would be able to share important information as to her mental state. It can be noted here that the focus was on understanding her experience, rather than on **pursuing an inquiry outside of her experience.** Even though Ms. P.'s wondering what to say ("I don't know what to say . . .") could be seen as an invitation for me to ask specific questions to obtain specific information, I was able to maintain my experience-near focus.

I said, "So many things to think about." Ms. P. at first did not seem to hear what I said. For some moments, without blinking, she stared into my eyes as if she were trying to come to some decision but having great difficulty in doing so. Then Ms. P. slowly nodded her head up and down to indicate that she agreed with my understanding. She said nothing but began to cry softly, and then sadly turned her head and fixed her gaze on a small painting of a snow scene hanging on the wall. She said, "How peaceful that is. I would like to be in that painting – to be painted in – a new world – a new place."

I sensed that Ms. P. was feeling relief and some excitement. The heaviness that I had picked up before had disappeared. Following her experience, I attempted to capture as much as possible the quality of the relief and excitement in her thinking in order to communicate as full an understanding as I could.

As previously stated, some patients may respond negatively to the therapist's understanding even though the communication of this understanding is directed only to that experience which is considered to be in the patient's ascendancy. However, in most instances the more complete the understanding provided by the therapist, the more the patient feels understood and motivated to share his or her thoughts in greater detail and depth. This, of course, facilitates the treatment process, and can make possible the necessary in-depth dynamic, economic, and genetic interpretations.

I responded in turn, "Like a tremendous burden lifted from your shoulders in thinking about being in the world of the painting." Ms. P., still looking at the painting, said (projecting some feeling of discouragement), "Yes – but more than tremendous – it's unbearable."

My understanding had fallen short of the true extent of her intensity and despair. Ms. P. had corrected my understanding by sharing with me a dimension of her feeling state which I had not picked up. This mutual sharing is an example of the intersubjective interchange which was earlier discussed. I shared my understanding of what I thought was going on with her. She accepted my understanding of her experience in part, and then with some discouragement added the dimension that I had missed. I postulated that Ms. P. was evidencing some capacity to accept my attempts to understand, was feeling somewhat discouraged when I did not fully understand, and was suffering intensely. I wished to communicate my new understanding, keeping in mind what I considered to be her experience in ascendancy, which was her discouragement at my inaccurate response.

I said, "I see, much more than just a burden – maybe it feels a little hopeless that I could fully understand." Ms. P. again began to cry softly and said, "It is hopeless. I don't think I can go on living in this world. I never thought I could think these things. It was never like me to get this far down. I never told anyone just how far down I am – like it came over me little by little until I feel too far down to ever come up or want to come up."

Ms. P. was vividly sharing with me her conviction of hopelessness about living. Unlike Ms. O., who, even though despairing, was motivated to try and make a difference in her life, Ms. P. was experiencing a kind of resignation, a sense of inevitability that things were all over for her.

Her trusting me with the seriousness of her situation was evidence of her ability to accept my continued attempts at understanding her. My picking up her correction and her hint of discouragement at my partial inaccuracy was pivotal in communicating to her my efforts at wishing and caring to know all of what she was feeling and thinking. It was after this intervention that Ms. P. allowed me to know fully what was going on. She furthered my understanding of the seriousness of her condition. At the same time, I suspected that I could sense – in her willingness to share – some slight hope in her that she believed I might understand her.

Ms. P. was communicating to me what might be a serious and potentially life-threatening emotional condition. However, at this point, she seemed too despairing to consider it worthwhile to speak further about her situation. **It was, therefore, important that I directly question her as to whether or not she had suicidal thoughts.**

I asked, "Are you saying you are considering not going on with your life?" Ms. P. unhesitatingly said, "Yes, I have made up my mind." She paused, was silent for some seconds, and then went on to say, "Before I came today I filled a prescription for sleeping pills which Dr. X. [the referring physician] had given me. I've decided to take them all tonight." She began to cry. "I can't believe I am saying these things. I can't believe that I can actually plan to take my life. It's just that the pain and loneliness are too much. I'm more afraid to live – but bringing this out into the open I think I'm afraid to die too. I don't think I thought about being afraid to die because of all that has happened. It's useless to talk about it – to think about it. I don't know why I came here."

At this point, direct questioning evolved from the patient's experience and was a necessary part of furthering my understanding.

I was now aware that Ms. P. had made plans for taking her life. I also understood that while she had shown a capacity to accept my attempts at understanding her, her pervasive experience of hopelessness was the dominant experience as confirmed by her concluding statement, "I don't know why I came here." I wished to communicate my limited understanding: (1) that she was experiencing overwhelming feelings of hopelessness that outweighed what beginning feelings of hope she might have had during our discussion, and (2) that I was aware that her overwhelming feelings of hopelessness were dictating to her that it was useless to think of going on with her life. I thought that these aspects were within Ms. P.'s preconscious or conscious awareness ("in ascendancy").

I said, "It seems useless coming here, like all hope in talking is lost in the face of your feelings." Ms. P. said, "Yes, I can't believe that there is any hope in talking. What good is it – like throwing a pebble in the ocean."

I got the impression that Ms. P., while deeply despairing, was again able to accept my understanding and to some limited extent was at least considering the question of whether or not talking could be of help. I sensed again that faint hint of her hope of being understood, which I had wondered about previously after she corrected my understanding of the extent of her despair.

I said, "Maybe you're not one hundred percent convinced that talking doesn't help – at least there is the pebble." For the first time in the session, Ms. P.'s sadness lessened. Her facial expression relaxed, and I thought I saw the beginnings of a smile. She said, "Maybe a pebble."

I said, "I know right now the pebble does not seem like much against these terrible feelings but perhaps it is a start." After some reflection, she responded, "I would say 'yes' now but I have no way of knowing about tonight." I said, "I know from you how powerful your feelings can get. To give the pebble a chance it is important that you not be unfairly tempted by the sleeping pills."

In summary, Ms. P. agreed that she should not take the sleeping pills home. She would keep only enough for one dosage to get her through the night and throw the rest away, which she did in my office. She also agreed to accept a referral that afternoon to a consulting psychiatrist, who would evaluate her regarding her need for medication and confer with me regarding his findings.* I made an appointment to see Ms. P. the following day, at which time she decided to begin treatment.

The direct questioning of Ms. P. emerged from and was directed to understanding her experience. This form of questioning, which can be defined as empathic experience-near questioning, should be differentiated from experience-distant questioning which does not emerge from the experience of the patient and which is not designed to further the understanding of the patient's moment-to-moment experiences. Experience-distant questioning imposes a direction of response and thereby runs the risk of recreating and perpetuating unempathic situations similar to those suffered by patients in the past. It is recognized, however, that experience-distant questioning may be required to obtain specific developmental information, and details regarding current and past behavior, in order to satisfy specific legal and/or insurance regulations.

---

*See E. S. Wolf (1988) for a discussion regarding the use of medication with disturbed patients.

CHAPTER 14

Development of the

Therapeutic Process:

The Case of Ms. O.

The following session with Ms. O. took place in the seventh month of her treatment. This session is highlighted here to show the development of the treatment process. Again, I have attempted to share my moment-to-moment thinking and experience with the reader, as well as to point out my theoretical understanding.

Ms. O. had increased her sessions to twice per week at the end of the third month of treatment, at which time she began to use the couch (lying down) rather than sitting. Her decision to use the couch came about after discussing its value and from her motivation to get in touch with deeper levels of her experience.

USE OF THE COUCH*

Ms. O.'s decision to use the couch came about from her motivation to get in touch with repressed memories and experiences, which she was better able to do when lying down.

It is well known that using the couch as a therapeutic tool does limit face-to-face eye contact with the analyst, and thereby is conducive to regressions to early affect states and to the recovery of what has been repressed. Patients who are severely disturbed—that is, who have serious defects in the self structure—can suffer breakup or disintegration of the self when in deeply regressed states as a result of the revival of the experiences, memories (screen), and fantasies surrounding childhood traumas. It is important, therefore, that the use of the couch be limited to those patients with sufficient cohesiveness in their self structure to tolerate the revival of past traumatic experiences. Through continuous empathic immersion into the patient's experience, the therapist can gain the information needed to make this determination. It is important that he or she determine the time of the onset of self defects, the areas and seriousness of these defects, the level of anxiety, and the potential for the development of compensatory structure, in order to best evaluate the extent of pathology and whether or not using the couch is advisable.

Factors that warn against the use of the couch can sometimes be immediately determined from the experience of the patient in the initial session. For example, if the patient is currently experiencing intense levels of hopelessness or reactive

---

*The much-debated issue regarding use of the couch, as it relates to the frequency of sessions and depth of treatment, will not be taken up here.

depression as was Ms. P., or if the patient has a history of severe depression, using the couch in the beginning of treatment would not be advisable. The same would hold true with patients who were experiencing a high level of anxiety as a reaction to current precipitating factors, or with those patients who have had a history of experiencing chronic debilitating anxiety. As the structure-building process takes place in the course of treatment, the advisability of the use of the couch can be re-evaluated.

A SYNOPSIS OF THE BEGINNING OF TREATMENT

By the seventh month of treatment, Ms. O. did not experience any of the physical symptoms she had reported in her initial sessions. She was now attending night school to get her high school equivalency diploma and had begun working part time during the day as a saleswoman in a clothing store. By means of the working-through of her early resistance to the emergence of the selfobject transferences, Ms. O. had gradually moved from her fixation on primitive idealizations to experiencing me as a more mature (idealized) selfobject who was empathically understanding, rather than a magically all-wise figure with whom she felt diminished. This movement can be understood as an unfolding and development of the idealizing selfobject transference as a result of the progress of treatment, which has been deepened through the total empathic process that includes understanding and explaining. Within this stable idealizing selfobject transference Ms. O. was also beginning to express a newfound assertiveness. There was a greater freedom to express exhibitionistic needs with me in the treatment, and with her husband. The beginning of the emergence of heretofore disavowed grandiose needs was signaled by a series of dreams in which she performed physical feats such as swimming across a surging river and leaping from one precipice to another.

A SESSION IN THE SEVENTH MONTH

Ms. O. walked slowly to the couch and lay down. She was silent for some time. She said, "I don't know what to say. My mind seems blank." She was silent for several minutes, apparently struggling with her thoughts. I said, "It's hard to get started today."

This communication of my understanding of her experience seemed to ease her tension. The therapeutic sequence of this opening moment began with my thinking and feeling my way into Ms. O.'s experience. It can be noted that my empathic focus was on her experience of not knowing what to say and her mind being "blank." I did not focus on trying to understand her from an experience-distant vantage point, questioning her as to what she meant by being "blank," for example, or asking what that was like for her, or asking her for associations to being blank in an effort to promote the revival of whatever repressed fantasies, thoughts, affects, and/or conflicts might be linked to the conscious and preconscious thought or experience of blankness. As has been stated, experience-distant questioning imposes upon the patient a direction of exploration that is outside the patient's experience.

My immersion into Ms. O.'s experience informed me that she was uneasy and was struggling with her thoughts. This data or information now formed the basis on which understanding, the first therapeutic unit in my treatment sequence, could be formulated. My understanding that Ms. O. was struggling with her thoughts was limited to the bit of information she provided, and subject to correction by Ms. O.

The reader may wonder how such a limited bit of information could be given so much attention. How could it be that important when there are so many complexities in a person's mental life? The answer is that these beginning experiences not only provide data but are also opportunities for the patient to feel immediately understood by the analyst. This facilitates the treatment process from the start of the session. Frequently, patients who do not feel understood at the beginning of a session carry over their sense of being misunderstood throughout the session. This can occur even though the analyst may become sensitively tuned in to the patient's ongoing experiences after the opening moments. Patients may acknowledge that "something is missing" or "wrong." There is a lackluster feeling about the session. A common complaint is that the patient feels distant or "not with it today." These nuances of feeling misunderstood from the beginning of the session can sometimes be difficult to detect until the session is well underway. When they are finally picked up, the patient will usually shift the focus of the session to that aspect of the experience that was missed. Patients sometimes, in coming to an awareness of the missing aspect of their experience late in the session, may feel considerable disappointment. They may even feel that the entire session was a waste of time. Therefore, it is important for the analyst to attempt to understand the nuances of the patient's experience as quickly and fully as possible.

"PERFECT EMPATHY"–NOT A GOAL

It is not our intention to imply that a new or seasoned analyst should strive for or be able to achieve a "perfect" state of empathic attunement. We would like to underscore that there is no such thing as perfect empathy. Analysts who feel the need to be perfectly attuned to their patients usually have difficulties. Their striving for such a goal tends to place them in a ritualistic straight jacket that inhibits their natural empathic capacities. In addition, they are likely to communicate their perfectionistic strivings to their patients. When the inevitable failures of empathy occur, these analysts are likely to blame themselves in some way, to be apologetic, and perhaps to strive more strongly for perfection. As a consequence, the analysis of the patient's disillusionment with the idealized selfobject analyst is likely to be undermined. For example, patients may be inhibited from expressing their disillusionment as they sense the extreme importance that being perfectly attuned has for the analyst. For many patients who suffered traumatic disappointments in the idealized parent and were unable to express their hurt and disillusionment, treatment would merely be a replay of those childhood traumas.

Also, the analyst who strives for perfect attunement holds out to his or her patients the illusion that their childhood hopes for the "perfect parent" can come true. This condition can result in the patient becoming what is commonly referred to as "addicted" to the analysis. Attempts by analysts to be perfect in their empathic attunement can result from a misunderstanding of self psychology theory and from unconscious (countertransference) archaic forms of grandiose strivings.

The second therapeutic unit in this sequence was my explanation of my understanding that Ms. O. was struggling with her thoughts. I sensed that her struggle was the experience in ascendancy. My communication, "It's hard to get started today," acknowledged that she was experiencing some inhibiting force (resistance) which was making it difficult for her to organize her thoughts and thus begin speaking.

RESISTANCE IN SELF PSYCHOLOGY

Ms. O.'s fears and anxieties at the moment she felt assertive, as I observed in the initial session, can be considered to be resistances in that they interfered with her emerging grandiose self and mirroring needs. As we have discussed, resistances and defenses are a necessary part of the treatment process; they are attempts by the psyche to protect the self from further narcissistic injury through revival of the memories, experiences, and fantasies of actual traumatic situations in the past. **Furthermore, resistances may also protect against the diffuse anxiety associated with every anticipated danger.** For example, Ms. O.'s momentarily experiencing assertiveness, at times during the initial session, threatened her not only with the recalling of actual traumatic rejections from her childhood (which she spoke of toward the end of the session); she was threatened also with the potentiality of facing further analogous traumas if she were to continue to assert her resentments and her ideas as an adult.

Attunement to the patient's experience is, therefore, important in determining the strength and nature of the resistances, and this determination becomes part of the understanding communicated to the patient. As with all explaining, the understanding that is communicated is determined by the extent of the patient's attunement to that which is in ascendancy. Whereas each patient's readiness and capacity for understanding is unique, there is frequently an observable sequence in the developing awareness of resistances. For example, (1) the patient comes to an understanding that there are times when he experiences some form of difficulty in carrying on the treatment. The difficulty may be experienced in a variety of ways – feeling unable to organize his thoughts, forgetting what was previously important, feeling disinterested and bored, feeling anxious and apprehensive, and the like; (2) he or she understands that his experiences of difficulty occur as a result of reactions (defensive) to specific experiences within the treatment and/or in his general life situation; and (3) he or she realizes that these times of difficulty are as important a part of the treatment as are other experiences,

and that they offer valuable opportunities for deepening understanding and therefore advancing the analytic process.

There may also be times when patients undergo intense
negative reactions to experiencing themselves differently, as well
as to their growing awareness of what happened to them as
children. Justifiable resentment of past traumas, along with a
desire to move toward the fulfillment of previously inhibited
ambitions and goals, can be highly threatening. This is especially
true if there has been a childhood history of traumatic rejection of
the patient's selfobject needs, and, in addition, if there is a
potential for similar rejections in the patient's current life situation should changes be made (e.g., the real possibility of a
spouse's rejection or the loss of a job). In these cases resistance to
treatment may not be experienced as a difficulty to be analyzed;
rather the patient may experience, as did Ms. P., the conviction
that it is useless to continue. As with Ms. P., it is important that
the analyst remain attuned to the patient's conviction of the
uselessness of treatment in order to gain an understanding of the
scope of the patient's hopelessness in going on with the treatment; to communicate an understanding of the scope of the
patient's experience; and to help the patient to feel understood. If
the patient can experience being understood (which is more
likely if the extent of the analyst's understanding of the patient's
experience is communicated), there can be a reduction of the
patient's anxieties and fears as the anxiety-relieving functions
of the analyst are internalized and as the self-selfobject tie is
strengthened.

My understanding that Ms. O. was experiencing a resistance to
speaking ("It's hard to get started today") had meaning for her. She said,
"Yes, I am feeling a lot right now but there seems to be something in
the way of my feeling free to speak my thoughts. It is strange because
I don't really feel any nervousness—just a general feeling of apprehen-

sion. It would be great to just start in fresh with your ideas without worry." She paused. "I don't think my new sales job will be that difficult."

Ms. O. had not told me of any new job. In retrospect, I felt that possibly her resistance in the opening of the session might have been related to her achievement in finding a new job, an achievement that, in turn, led to the assumption that I knew. In other words, the assumption that I already knew of her new job made it unnecessary for her to speak about her success.

Here, Ms. O. was using denial as a major defense mechanism to protect her enfeebled self against the diffusive anxiety and anticipated dangers associated with exposing her abilities, strengths, and capacity to achieve (i.e., exposure of the grandiose self). From our work I had already obtained a general understanding that she had been repeatedly scorned and humiliated as a child and as an adolescent whenever she made attempts to express her point of view or to gain approval for her achievements. Ms. O.'s developing grandiose self and her need for validation as competent, worthwhile, and important had been seriously undermined by the time she was 3. She described the many paralyzing moments of fear when, as a child, she and her siblings had been left alone by their parents for days on end. Ms. O. remembered the neighbors who were kind and who cared for them at those times. Their kindness, however, did not relieve the fear that something might happen to her. She alluded to many such moments of terror which she had experienced throughout her childhood, trying to survive in a chaotic and depressing environment.

I said, "You thought that I knew about your new job?" She said with surprise, "I told you. Oh no, I did not tell you. That's right, I only found out about it after our last session." I was aware that she was experiencing considerable anxiety. She was restless and tense. Then there was a noticeable shift in her mood to a feeling of sadness as she suddenly switched topics. "I keep remembering a story I heard when I was 12 – two little girls I knew from the neighborhood were brutally shot and killed – it's been on my mind for a long time – I've always wondered how the parents felt." She began to cry softly. Sensing her sadness, I said, "Really horrible!" She said, "Yes, I still can't believe it – no one knows what happened – out of the blue – you're here and then you're gone."

Ms. O. went on to describe her relationship with the children. She knew one of them. She spoke wistfully of her, feeling that the little girl was exactly like the one she would like to have someday. Ms. O.'s sadness diminished considerably as she continued to share her intense emotions and her hopes for having a child of her own one day.

I was able to maintain my experience-near attunement with Ms. O.'s experience of remorse even though I felt upset at hearing the story of the shootings. I felt curious and was tempted to ask for more of the details. To do so, however, would have interfered with her need to share her experience with regard to the tragedy and her wish to be a mother. As with Ms. P., direct questioning which promotes the understanding of the patient's experience is sometimes necessary. **However, direct questioning which arises out of, and for the purpose of satisfying, the therapist's personal needs becomes an experience-distant intrusion and an interruption in the development of the selfobject transferences.**

Being in her experience, I was able to capture the depth of her feeling regarding the tragedy. It was not only the tragic death that was deeply upsetting to her, but it was also the circumstances surrounding the shooting. The children were suddenly and shockingly murdered – here one moment and then dead – without anyone knowing what had happened.

I was aware that Ms. O. began thinking of the tragedy immediately after she remembered that she had not told me of her success. I understood this as a way her mind was dealing with the anxiety over her success. Her own expectation of disaster, which was triggered by her success at acquiring work, took the form of the memory of the tragic shooting. Kohut (1971) describes this process, the "telescoping of genetically analogous experiences" (p. 53), as an attempt to express earlier traumas through later ones that are similar or analogous to them. The overlaying of past experiences with more recent ones is not necessarily an attempt to ward off repressed memories; rather the later experiences are closer to consciousness and can therefore be more easily communicated.

The mind has the ability to do this through its capacity to combine or synthesize thoughts, ideas, fantasies, and experiences into a different complex whole. One might wonder what experience or experiences in Ms. O.'s past could possibly be analogous to her experience of the actual shooting of two children.

During the seven months of treatment I had learned that Ms. O. had not experienced in the past any tragedies similar to the one she described with the children. However, her experience of the shooting of the children was not unlike the sudden and paralyzing moments already described when she was abandoned by her parents, as well as the life-threatening jeopardy she had continuously suffered in the ghetto environment.

A major consideration here is that one does not need to have undergone a life situation similar to another person's to have experiences that are similar.

Through Ms. O.'s telling me of the shootings, I was able to get a more specific sense of how intensely she felt about the tragedy – its suddenness and unpredictability, which she related to life in general. I wished to communicate my understanding, which included an awareness of the heightened intensity of her feelings and the dread-filled expectations at taking a new job, all of which I saw as crystallized in the tragedy of the children.

I said, "You began to think about what happened to the children when you realized that I had not known of your new job." Ms. O. angrily responded, "Don't remind me of my new job." She became quiet; she seemed sad and tearful. She added, "I almost feel I can't breathe." Ms. O. suddenly sat up and began to inhale deeply. She then lay back on the couch and for some moments was quiet.

I was surprised at the intensity of her reaction. It was apparent that she did not feel understood. I therefore questioned my intervention, and it then occurred to me that I had ignored an important aspect of her experience that was in ascendancy; that is, her hopefulness of one day having a child of her own. I wondered why I had not stayed with this aspect of her experience, even though her shift from thinking of the new job to thinking of the tragedy of the children was an important dynamic to be understood. I concluded that my unconscious need (countertransference) for Ms. O. to analyze her inhibiting fears prevented me from making the shift to her happy and hopeful experience of being a mother.

Ms. O.'s sadness and silence indicated that my intervention had created a disruption in the empathic idealizing selfobject bond. I wished to explain to her what I understood had happened, so that the treatment could be set back on course and the selfobject tie repaired.

I said, "I think that I upset you by shifting gears away from what was important to you. You were speaking about how wonderful it would be to have a child." Ms. O. began to nod her head, indicating she agreed with my understanding. After several seconds she said, "Like always—

you too – cold water being thrown on my hopes. Being a mother was something beautiful that my mother always talked about. It gave me hope. But that was spoiled when I realized that my mother was trapped by one birth after another. She could go nowhere with her life. I think I remember the hopelessness – I think I feel it right now – like I'm sinking – back into the helpless position where everyone knows more than I do. It's miserable, but like we've said, it's safe. Nobody says I'm stupid there. It's like being stupid already – like a foregone conclusion." She paused and for a moment began to cry softly. I feel like when I was little – everybody had a routine – something horrible happened if you stepped out of line – like Donald Duck's nephews who never said a full sentence – each could say only one word – until all the one words made a sentence. I don't think any of them knew what the sentence was until all the words were said.

Ms. O. felt understood by my intervention that explained why she was upset (". . . by shifting gears away from what was important . . .") and thereby disillusioning her as had her mother. It can be noted here that she associated her disillusionment with me as an idealized selfobject to the experience of disillusionment with her mother without my making a genetic interpretation. We suggest that patients will frequently do so if the moment-to-moment dynamics of the selfobject transference are understood and communicated. It is acknowledged that issues around interpretations in self psychology are complex ones requiring a broader elaboration than can be offered here. For now, however, it can be suggested that allowing patients to make "their own interpretations" and reconstructions is an important consideration in the explaining process that the treatment depends upon.

For example, I was not aware of the extent of Ms. O.'s idealization of her mother and her disillusionment with her. I was, however, aware of her disillusionment with her father as she had previously spoken of many experiences related to that. If, in my explaining, I had gone beyond the immediacy of my empathic failure and the disruption of the idealizing selfobject bond, and had interpreted her disillusionment with me as analogous to that experienced with her father, I might have limited her in her own exploration and interpretative efforts.

It can also be pointed out that Ms. O. explored the intensity (economic) of her experience of disillusionment ("I feel helpless ... like I am sinking ...") as well as the regressive retreat (dynamic) to the primitive idealizing bond ("... back in the helpless position where everyone knows more than I do ") without specific efforts on my part to interpret these components which again may have limited her efforts at understanding.

Ms. O. seemed deep in thought. Then with a start, she said, "Oh, my God, I just remembered I have an exam tonight and I forgot all about it. It's like too many good things are happening. I'm leaving my stupidity behind. My husband says I am spending too much time away from home. I'm embarrassing him. He said I don't need a career–he is the provider of the family–maybe he is right–I should quit and stay home–like the wife he said he married–it's like I betrayed him. He'll find other women to satisfy him." She began to cry audibly. "I don't know why I am crying. You know my mind just went to the two little girls who were shot! Guess I feel that I am going to die too if I go on." Ms. O. abruptly stopped speaking and became visibly anxious. She began to breath rapidly but remained lying on the couch.

Again, Ms. O. remembered the murder of the children when she began thinking of herself as achieving. This time, however, she was able to make the connection between her thinking about the children and her feeling that she will die if she continues to achieve.

It can be suggested that Ms. O. was able to consider the genetic ramifications of her disillusionment as well as to recognize the connection between the progress she has made and her feelings of dying, as a result of being understood and the reestablishment of the sustaining idealizing selfobject transference. It is also important to note that as the transmuting internalization structure-building process continued, Ms. O. was able to recover for the first time a positive idealizing experience with her mother. It can be further noted that even though a patient may have a pervasive, unempathic selfobject milieu, such as that of Ms. O., which results in fixations on archaic configurations, even within such a generally unempathic environment there can be transitory positive selfobject experiences which serve as prototypes that can be recovered and built upon in the treatment. This consideration may have significant implications for the treatment of the severely disturbed patient population.

I was aware that during these months of treatment Ms. O. had shown a considerable ability to reveal and analyze details of past frightening and saddening experiences. As stated, developmentally she was moving away from her archaic form of idealization which consisted of her as a mindless servant to the powerful figure who would punish her if she did not obey. Within the context of her developing idealizing selfobject transference with me, she was now facing primitive fears of destroying and being destroyed which inhibited the unfolding of her grandiose self.

I wished to communicate my understanding that she was allowing herself to go forward in her understanding of herself in the face of intense anxiety and discomfort. As with previous interventions, this communication recognized her emerging grandiose self and had the effect of facilitating the development of the mirror transference and internalization (transmuting internalization) of the functions of the analyst. More specifically I wished to communicate my awareness of her ability to explore the genetic connections of her disillusionment, as well as her awareness of her expectation of dying, should she continue her progress.

I said, "You have tied together the hopeless feeling you experienced with me to that which you experienced with your mother. I get a better idea of the pervasive feeling of constriction you suffered as a little girl, and the fear now when you think of your progress." With a sense of alertness and aliveness she responded, "You know I really believe this position that everyone knows more than I do keeps me safe when I think of going forward. I guess going forward means being alone–so alone–alone like in a shock with no relief–I can't really put it into words."

Ms. O. began to shift her body anxiously as if she was unable to find a comfortable position. She said, "I feel like sitting up but I won't." She crossed her legs and then folded her arms tightly over her chest, and said, "I can't conceive of this full-time position being for me or school being for me. Those things are meant only for my husband. That's weird to say that. Each step I take I feel like taking cover. It boils down to this: If I'm not stupid, something is going to happen." Ms. O. suddenly raised both of her knees. Her arms remained folded in the same manner.

Attempting to maintain my immersion into her experience, I increasingly sensed a mounting physical tension of which I felt she was also aware (in ascendancy). I sensed she was holding herself even more rigidly as if she were guarding against something. I wished to communicate my understanding that she was expressing herself physically.

I said, "I sense you're feeling an awful lot right now, as if somehow you're physically protecting yourself." Ms. O. quickly responded, "It's true I'm aware of holding myself tight. Well, I said I couldn't put things into words. I know something is wrong right now, but I don't believe anyone could understand me and especially my words."

Ms. O. seemed to relax somewhat but remained in her protective position on the couch. I was aware that this was the first time in the months of treatment that she was considering her disbelief that someone could understand her.

She continued, "I don't think I was supposed to speak. Yes, I do remember that I learned to be quiet."

Ms. O. began to cry and recounted times when she was about 4. She would lie awake at night in the same bed with her three older sisters. Frequently, she had wet the bed. She remembered feeling "frozen" with fear – as if the night were a person – a giant who could make sounds but could not be seen. She dared not speak. She would purposely move around in the bed until her sisters awoke and screamed at her. She almost welcomed the screams because they would "take away the night." Nobody knew of her fears. She said that I was the only one she had ever told. I was the only person who had ever understood her.

CHAPTER 15

More Specific
Understanding: The Case
of Ms. O.

As exemplified in the preceding session, Ms. O.'s ability to make a connection between her fear of dying and going ahead with her goals was a major step in leading to a more detailed understanding of the relationship of her current anxieties and fears of assertiveness and exhibitionism with past traumas. It was also a major step in eventually leading to a more specific understanding of the relationship of these fears and anxieties to her regressive retreats to subservient idealization.

SOME DEVELOPMENTAL HISTORY

In time Ms. O. was able to explore the particulars of the early traumas and the time periods in which they occurred. For example, it was learned through her memory of what she was told, her own associations, and reconstructions of what took place that Ms. O.'s suffering began when she was between approximately 2 and 3 years old. She was the youngest of six children, with three sisters and two brothers. All were one year apart in age except for herself; she was born three years after the fifth child. The family lived in a small two-room apartment. Ms. O. and her sisters slept together in a single bed next to her brothers who slept in an adjoining bed in the same room. Her mother and father slept in a separate bed in the same room as the children.

Ms. O., as were all of the children, was breast-fed until approximately 2 years of age. She slept alone with her mother until she was approximately 3 years of age, at which time she was placed in the bed to sleep with her sisters. Ms. O. was later told that, when that happened, she cried for hours at night and wet the bed. She could be comforted only if her mother slept with her. She was then put to bed at an earlier time and left alone to exhaust herself with crying before falling off to sleep.

Ms. O.'s earliest memories are of the times when she awakened at night in fear. There was a recurrent childhood dream of being chased by an unrecognizable animal. She remembered the sounds of her mother and father having sexual intercourse, which confused her and paralyzed her with fear. She recalled that by the age of 7 she would masturbate compulsively when she awoke. She had the fantasy at those times that masturbation allowed her body to relax. Her thought was that she could not extend her arms and legs without it. Beginning with preadolescence the theme of her fantasies was being masturbated by a threatening male figure who was dangerous to others but kind to her as long as she did what he wanted. Her bed-wetting and masturbation continued until she was 13, at which time she went to live with a number of different relatives in a neighboring city. She was puzzled by the fact that she then stopped wetting the bed and masturbating daily, but thought it was because her fear and anxieties had subsided when she left home. A short time later she left to travel and get whatever jobs she could to support herself.

Ms. O. remembered both her mother and father as being subservient. Her mother was experienced as being dominated by her father who "always came first no matter what." On the other hand, her father, who worked as a handyman for a housing complex, was always willing to do anything his bosses asked him even if it went beyond his regular duties, and even if it was without pay. She described him as tyrannical with her mother and the children but weak when it came to standing up for himself outside the family.

Ms. O. remembered her disdain for both her parents and her disappointment with them from an early age. She described herself as the only one of the children who seemed to see or care about what was going on. Perhaps because she was the youngest she was able to get more positive attention from her sisters and brothers, and was able to avoid the brunt of her father's harsh and controlling demands.

There was little or no recognition by either parent of the wishes of any of the children to pursue independent and autonomous interests. Two of her sisters showed unusual talent in drawing and painting, but were not allowed to take instruction even though it had been offered by a local artist without cost to the family. Ms. O. described many such instances in which she and her siblings were not only inhibited from participating in activities but discouraged from even speaking about their hopes and dreams. Ms. O. came to recognize in her treatment that her mother and father were fearful people who had been thwarted in their own development. Nevertheless, there were times of happiness and enjoyment when her parents showed concern and love. But her disillusionment with her parents intensified as she saw her brothers and sisters "give up on life." All of them, including Ms. O., dropped out of school in their early teens and left home either to work or to live with relatives.

Ms. O.'s traumatic disillusionment began in the preoedipal period and extended through the oedipal. The drive-channeling and self-soothing functions of the idealized selfobject, which are normally accrued during the preoedipal period, were incomplete, thereby leaving her extremely vulnerable to the relentless unempathic and sexually overstimulating environment. The development of a system of values which provide hope and direction for a worthwhile future was seriously undermined. In general, her childhood experiences left her confused and in danger of giving up on life. She left home, as did her brothers and sisters, to salvage what was left of her hopes for some fulfillment of her many unmet needs. As a result of her many disillusioning traumas, she became developmentally fixed on a primitive and infantile yearning for the perfect godlike idealized figure who would protect, lead, and direct her. This yearning led her to an early marriage to her controlling and directing husband who fit the primitive idealized image she sought. In effect, Ms. O. was trapped in a primitive selfobject bond. Though she was anxious, depressed, and physically in pain, she could not extricate herself because the grandiose/exhibitionistic self was also severely undermined and fixated in a primitive form.

Her natural childhood wish to exhibit and assert herself was not tolerated. She recalled no severe spankings nor any other physical abuse during her childhood. However, she remembered that when she was assertive, expressing her thoughts and will fulness, there was a cold and distant look on her father's face. It was his "looking through her" that frightened her. Ms. O. experienced these moments as "warnings of doom" and "looks of a killer." Her most fearful associations were to her repeated childhood experience of hearing her mother and father during sexual intercourse – the unbearable overstimulation, the confusion as to whether her mother was being killed, the frightening sounds, and her own uncontrolled bed-wetting and masturbation that led to an overall experience of helplessness, vulnerability, and aloneness. For the most part, Ms. O. suffered the extreme of what Kohut has referred to as a dehumanized environment in which there is a cold indifference to the self of another. This leads to overwhelming anxiety, loss of identity, and disintegration experiences.

For her, it seemed that she was trapped in a life circumstance filled with inevitable dangers. To be silent was to face the unchecked relentless indifference to which she was subjected, and with it an intolerable disintegration anxiety. On the other hand, to assert herself and complain was to invite further disdain and indifference.

Her childhood fantasy of being physically hurt or destroyed in some way should she dare to be assertive, was exacerbated by her mother's inability to provide an understanding of what she as a young girl was experiencing; Ms. O. fruitlessly attempted to discuss this with her over and over again.

FEARS OF DEATH AND ANNIHILATION

Ms. O. had remained fixed on a primitive and magical notion that one can physically destroy or be destroyed through looks, words, and thoughts. Her primitive idealization – subservience to the omnipotent all-powerful figure – offered her the only hope of survival.*

As treatment progressed, her fear of being physically destroyed should she be assertive was understood as the paralyzing effects of disintegration anxiety experiences, which as a child she had interpreted as her body being destroyed. As these fears were explored and slowly worked through, their intensity diminished. She was able to finish her course work and pass her high school equivalency examination during the second year of treatment. She had succeeded in her job as a saleswoman in a large department store, and during the third year of treatment was promoted to assistant manager in one of the store's departments that had a large Hispanic customer population **Each step of her success triggered severe anxiety and the familiar conviction that she would somehow die or be hurt.** These apprehensions were apparent in her dreams, which progressed from the vague dreams of being chased by animals to more delineated figures of male and female attackers who wished to kill her. A recurrent theme was being chased by different male figures with a knife. Her associations to the men usually were a composite of her father, husband, and myself. As she worked through the severity of her fears of destroying and of being destroyed, she was able to risk sharing repressed childhood exhibitionistic wishes and exposing unmet needs of mirroring within the context of the predominant idealizing selfobject transference. She was able to tolerate the inevitable disappointments in me when I was unable to meet her early

---

*It can also be noted that throughout treatment there was a minimum of twinship relatedness even with the sisters nearest in age. Ms. O. considered herself to have been a "loner" throughout her early schooling. In later grades she had formed brief sexual relationships with controlling young men. In my findings it is not unusual for individuals who have been severely traumatized in both the idealizing and grandiose sectors to have a limited twinship relatedness. These findings suggest that severe damage to these two sectors may inhibit twinship play, because twinship does entail experiencing aspects of exhibitionism and idealization.

thwarted needs for recognition when they went beyond the scope of analysis. For example, in the excitement of beginning her new job she wanted me to stop by her workplace (as it was in the neighborhood of my office) to see the many things she was doing. Another instance was her request to call me at any time she might wish, even though there was no emergency. In general, she wished me to be readily available to her as the admiring and appreciative mirroring parental selfobject of which she had been so severely deprived as a child.

THE THWARTED NEED FOR IDEALIZATION

Ms. O. was also able to tolerate her disillusionment with me at those times when she was aware that I could not provide the magical answers which would take away all her pain and make her life happy. For instance, she became frustrated with me in the initial months because she was convinced that I had "the answers" to her problems, but was simply refusing to reveal them to her. The tentative expression of her developing grandiose self triggered childhood expectations of being destroyed by powerful assaultive figures or being "overlooked" as if she did not exist. It was in the face of these fears that Ms. O. retreated to the more archaic form of idealization and wished me to give her magical answers and direction that would protect, comfort, and assure her.

It should be noted here that this primitive idealization of the powerful and all-knowing leader had sustained Ms. O. throughout the many successive traumatic, fragmenting experiences of her life. If I had failed to maintain an empathic immersion into the many nuances and aspects of her idealization, then more than likely I would not have been able to understand the vital importance and value that this idealizing experience provided for her. On the contrary, I might have viewed what emerged in the treatment as evidence of serious defects in her reality testing, and would have made attempts to correct her reasoning and so on. Or I might have viewed her initial subservience or frequent regressions merely as her defenses against repressed aggression, separation–individuation problems, and oedipal fears. I would, therefore, have insinuated that her need for idealization was faulty and should be changed.

If I had failed to comprehend from the beginning of treatment how her idealizing experience had provided her with the only avenue through which she could preserve an enfeebled self, I would have repeated the very same disillusioning experiences of which she now perceived herself a lifelong victim. I would have understood neither the importance of accepting her idealization of me, nor her inevitable disillusionments and frustrations when I failed to fulfill her hopes. Finally, I would not have been able to communicate an adequate enough understanding of her experience to enable her to feel understood, and her anxiety and frustration to be relieved. The process of transmuting the internalization of the analyst's empathic functions, which requires that frustration remain at a tolerable level, would have been seriously undermined.

DEVELOPMENT OF THE SELFOBJECT
TRANSFERENCES: A SUMMARY

In summarizing the emergence of the selfobject transferences in the case of Ms. O., we have chosen to focus upon the gradual movement away from fixations on her primitive forms of idealization to more developed levels, while at the same time showing the development of a stable mirror transference in the narrower sense. In this summary we also highlight the meaning these developments had for her life. As the working through of these developments took place, there was a gradual but noticeable improvement in all areas of her life.

Simply stated, Ms. O.'s progress in treatment could be described as her becoming increasingly more comfortable with her emerging grandiosity, as the transmuting internalization of the analyst's empathic anxiety-relieving functions took place through a sequence of working through tolerable disappointments and disillusionments with the analyst.

Except for periods of regression, she experienced me less and less as the all-wise leader who knew what direction she should take, and with whom she must be beholden and subservient. Rather, I began to be experienced more and more as a nondirective idealized figure who "put her first" by understanding and respecting the direction in which she wished to go. The vital importance that this developing idealizing experience had for Ms. O. was expressed in her wish "to stay in treatment forever." I was the only one who could understand her. She could never bear to leave treatment as she would then lose the revitalizing hope for life that she had gained there. Her idealization was not unlike that which could have been expected to develop with her parents, had her life circumstances been different. For example, it is normal for children to look up to and long to merge with idealized parental figures, whom they view as possessing unquestioned superior strength, power, intelligence, and love. The thought of separating from the idealized parents whether it be to attend school for the first time, to go off to summer camp, or to get married, can trigger painful feelings of loss. If the parents are attuned to these natural feelings of idealization, they can offer their children the support needed to seek out new and equally satisfying selfobject experiences. In this way the idealization of the parents becomes less exclusive as selfobject needs undergo developmental changes and new selfobjects are sought.

In treatment, the patient's emerging selfobject needs become concentrated in the selfobject transference. This is a result of an in-depth analytic understanding and explaining which, unlike the patient's life situation, allows for the unfolding of the thwarted needs of childhood. For example, Ms. O.'s idealizing transference developed from a relatively archaic to a more mature form after a painful working through of fears and anxieties arising from severe traumas of her childhood. The understanding that we came to was an in-depth analytic one which was exclusive to our treatment. It was an understanding that could not be expected to be provided by her husband, her friends, or anyone else within a social context. Therefore, Ms. O.'s feeling that I was the only one who had ever understood her was correct within the context of her generally unempathic history. It was also a realistic acknowledgment of the unique and special understanding which had actually occurred in the treatment. Ms. O.'s idealizing experience was one in which I, as the idealized selfobject, understood her more deeply and completely than did anyone else. She had repeatedly stated that the insights she gained in treatment made it possible for her to "have life." Without treatment she was certain that she would have been "a victim of her fears" and ended up like her brothers and sisters, who had never finished high school and were barely eking out an existence.

The development of the idealizing transference was a significant advancement in the treatment. Kohut, throughout his writings, has reminded the analyst of the importance of not interfering with the emergence of the selfobject transferences by attempting in some way to foster their development (for example, through encouragement or trying to be a "good selfobject" through some action or comment), or by interfering with their development by failing to accept them. For example, if I had some personal difficulty in being admired, I might have communicated my feelings of discomfort through some word or action which would have interrupted her idealization by implying that I was not as understanding as she thought.

INFLUENCING EFFECTS OF THE IDEALIZING SELFOBJECT TRANSFERENCE

Through the empathic immersion in the patient's experience the analyst can become clearer as to the meaning and consequences that these selfobject transferences have for the individual. For example, Ms. O.'s idealizing of me as the exclusive understanding selfobject was also inhibiting in that she began to ignore and devalue learning from others. Her wish to stay in analysis "forever" was based on her idealized impression of me as being the only one who could completely understand her. She began to complain that her husband's and friends' ideas about "life" were limited, compared to what she had discovered in treatment. For a brief time she considered divorcing her husband and leaving her job. She reasoned that her husband was not understanding enough to raise a child. Perhaps she should go back to school and become either a psychotherapist or a teacher.

In effect Ms. O. was concerned that there was very little to gain from her personal relationships and from her current administrative job position. The only worthwhile pursuit would be to stay in analysis forever and/or become associated with some related field. Ms. O.'s devaluation of her husband's and her friends' "way of thinking" was not defensive, because she was not avoiding anxiety-provoking thoughts or impulses, for example, through splitting of good and bad, self and object representations as object relations theory might suggest. Rather, Ms. O. was now experiencing long overdue, thwarted developmental demands for the enriching, self-soothing, and comforting functions which had been largely denied her by the idealized figures in her life. This was a major development. As sometimes happens, however, at such a point in treatment, this development overshadowed the value and importance of other learning experiences as well as other relationships.

It is important to reemphasize that this self psychological theoretical view of idealization was formulated from understanding the patient's experience. It is, therefore, experience-near and quite different from the traditional experience-distant view of idealization as a defensive and inhibiting process. The self psychological view of idealization opens the patient to a broader perspective of growth, in that the unfolding of the idealization goes beyond the selfobject analyst as the only source of understanding. Rather, the idealization unfolds to include the selfobject analyst's appreciation of the patient's ongoing opportunities for learning and being understood by other idealized figures outside the analysis. Without this awareness of the influence of the idealizing selfobject transference, and without this broader self psychological view of idealization, many patients can become stalemated in treatment. Frequently they look to their analysts as "gurus" and, as Ms. O. wished, give up their own direction in life to become followers of individuals or organizations, in a cult-like fashion without any serious thought about the limitations this places on their learning and growth. A consequence of these limiting experiences is that the development of all sectors of the self can be undermined. As the development of the idealization process remains limited, so will the opportunity for ongoing development of mature idealized selfobjects, and for the internalization of new values and goals. As sources of learning are narrowed, the patient's thoughts, ideas, and plans for future goals will be narrowed. Therefore, the development of the grandiose self, that sector of the self that organizes and puts ideas into action, will necessarily be constricted. This constriction, in turn, limits the potential for acquiring enhanced feelings of self-esteem. Finally, twinship needs for supportive like-minded people remain limited, and are therefore confined to a narrow, parochial range of selfobjects.

Having emphasized the importance of the influencing effects of the idealizing transference, I would like to continue to summarize the development of Ms. O.'s idealizing selfobject transference, and then highlight the moment-to-moment sequence of part of a session in the sixteenth month of treatment at which time Ms. O. communicated her desire to leave her husband, friends, and job to continue in treatment while pursuing a career relevant to her new understandings.

As the idealizing transference developed, Ms. O. began to acknowledge more and more the importance of "being understood" in the treatment. She felt that this understanding was allowing her to explore with greater depth and intensity the contrasting disillusionments of her childhood. In particular, she was able to get in touch with previously unacknowledged disillusionments with her father. She tearfully recalled feeling that she was special to him, during occasional family outings throughout her childhood. He played with her, carried her on his shoulders, and particularly on one occasion wove her a flower bracelet. However, when the family returned home, it was as if she did not exist. She wondered how could this have happened; it was as if he were two different people. As she explored the extent of her childhood disillusionments, she began to express disillusionment with her husband and friends.

In my work with Ms. O., I gradually came to learn that these current disillusioning experiences occurred mainly around specific situations and discussions in which she was able to express her opinion – usually in direct opposition to her husband and friends – about social issues. Ms. O. was, for the most part, disgusted with what she called the "depth of the discussion." By this she meant that her friends in general, and her husband in particular, had very little "understanding" for the plight of the disadvantaged; and that therefore their ideas seemed to her insensitive and superficial.

The increasing intensity of her disillusionment seemed to have originated with one particular discussion in which her husband made a number of racial and ethnic slurs against prominent politicians he personally knew. She felt some disappointment with him at first, but unlike other times the feeling persisted. Gradually over a period of weeks she experienced a "sickening" and "sinking" disillusionment with a number of acquaintances and friends.

At this period in the treatment her associations led to another childhood experience of disillusionment, this time in one of her older brothers whom she had "looked up to" for comfort and support. With some embarrassment she recalled her sense of betrayal and "total confusion" with him when she was around 5 or 6 years old, and he was 12. He usually comforted her at bedtime by reading her stories. On one particular night, however, he got into bed and began to touch her vagina. This recollection in turn, led her to remember many details of her experience of hearing her parents when they were having sexual intercourse. She remembered many of the words they spoke during intercourse and her feelings of confusion and fright. She was too frightened to say anything to her parents, not only about their sexual activity but also about her brother's molesting her and the fear that it might happen again. There was only one person she felt she could speak with, and that was her maternal aunt who lived nearby. Ms. O. described this aunt as "stern and mean" but as someone who would listen to her. She told her aunt about her brother, but she feared speaking about her parents as her aunt was very protective of her mother. The aunt did, however, intervene with her parents to protect her from her brother.

Ms. O.'s disillusionment with her husband and friends persisted until she began to consider leaving her marriage and her job to pursue the vague, undefined goal of her "psychological interests." It was in a session in the sixteenth month that she revealed the full extent of her disillusionment.

A SESSION IN THE SIXTEENTH MONTH

Ms. O. walked into her session somewhat more slowly than usual. She seemed preoccupied. As she lay on the couch, I experienced her as being very much alone with her thoughts. She said nothing for over a minute. I said, "You're feeling far away today." After some moments she said, "Yes, I don't feel well. I don't mean I'm physically feeling bad–just feeling bad in general. This is the only place I feel hopeful. I would like to stay here forever. What good is talking to people if everything is on the surface – if people can't understand on a deep level. You don't know how sick I feel when I hear my husband and friends talk about certain things. We went to dinner at a friend's last night. I couldn't believe the superficiality. My husband thought they were great. I'm thinking again–seriously this time–about divorce and leaving my job so I can put all my efforts into going to college."

As Ms. O. spoke, I sensed a determination and assertiveness which had not been evident initially in the session. I also sensed an intensity and depth of disillusionment not apparent in previous sessions, as well as a strength of conviction that it was necessary to leave her husband and job in order to pursue psychological studies. There was an all-or-nothing, cult-like attitude to her thinking. She seemed to be feeling that there was nothing worthwhile in her marriage or work. She was sharing with me a fuller expression of her disillusionment with most aspects of her life, except for treatment. As the session proceeded and she explored specifics of her childhood deprivations, she was able to experience more and more the extent of her painful disillusionments and disappointments. As she sensed my remaining empathically attuned through all these difficult moments, there seemed to be an even greater intensification of the idealizing selfobject transference. It was at this point that I wished to communicate my understanding: first, that she was feeling rewarded by her progress in treatment; and second, that she was feeling so disillusioned with her life outside of treatment that it could only have meaning if she remained in therapy "forever" and/or if she devoted herself to some form of related work.

I said, "I know how valuable our work has been for you. I think that the depth of analytic understanding you have gained makes other discussions seem superficial and worthless in comparison." Ms. O. seemed deep in thought and relaxed. After some moments she nodded her head in agreement. "I really feel our work has saved my life," she said. "I'm amazed how far I've come and how easy it is to be successful. Yes, I guess our work does have such meaning that anything else seems worthless including my husband. You know–he said last night that the reason people are poor is because they're lazy. Can you believe that?" She became silent for several seconds and then began to laugh. "I'm laughing because it was less than two years ago when I thought everybody was smarter." She paused again. "Guess I'm forgetting all the good things that I've had with Roberto [her husband]. He's really very smart in many ways and very successful. He's also been very good to me." Ms. O. began to cry softly. "I don't know why I'm crying. It's like more than I can hope for to think I can have what I've gained here and then have my husband too." I said, "It feels like you could not have both." She said, "Yes, I think I'm starting to feel anxious right now. I think I'm feeling like the religious people in the Bible who would not associate with sinners for fear of losing their purity of thought. I think I am feeling that way with Roberto. If he's not analytic, I might lose my good feeling about our work here. You know he does sometimes say to me that I should stop treatment. It's too expensive and things like that. You know, I think I'm afraid of slipping back to the old worship way where I'm the follower without a mind." I said, "I see what you mean, you might lose the hope and confidence you have gained in our work."

"Exactly," she responded. "I guess my hopes feel so new that they are still shaky. I need a protective environment to hold on to them. I'm still not certain that I can't be driven back by my husband's insensitive remarks–back into that old image of myself where my fantasy is that I'm worthless and he's everything. You know–it's not unlike being overlooked, and we know what that means. My heritage of being overlooked–a good name for a book. Yeah . . . chapter one, I Rode on His Shoulders and Disappeared in his Eyes–chapter two, From a Fairy Tale to a Finger in Mine–chapter three, Where Were You, Mommy Dearest? I have at least twelve more chapters. . . ."

Here is another example in which the analyst's remaining in the patient's moment-to-moment experience led to the patient's making genetic corrections in a more creative and encompassing way than, perhaps, the analyst could possibly conceive. Ms. O.'s fears in this session diminished as reconstructions were made – primarily by her–and as she experienced, explored, and analyzed even deeper feelings of sadness, bursts of rage, and justifiable anger at the pervasive deprivations she had suffered. In particular, specifics of situations were reconstructed in which her mother's passivity, fearfulness, and submissiveness to the father resulted in her pervasive indifference to Ms. O.

From this point, and as the working-through process continued, Ms. O. began to reevaluate the meaningfulness of her relationship with her husband. This was an important transitional step and an ongoing theme of the treatment, as was her sense that she had to restrict herself to the "protective environment" of the analytic process in order to maintain her idealized experience of hopefulness and inspiration. As treatment progressed, Ms. O. became more open to learning from many sources other than the analytic process.

By the third year in treatment, she had entered college and felt excited with this new phase in her life. She began to question her previously idealized experience of the understanding she had been gaining in treatment. Through her studies she became interested in various views and concepts of psychology. As she studied and as she spoke with her instructors she became aware of the diversity of theoretical explanations and ways of understanding human behavior. Her previously held idealized view of our way of understanding as the only way was challenged. While retaining a belief in our work, she experienced a bit-by-bit disillusionment with me as the all-knowing idealized selfobject. As the disillusionment progressed, the intensity of the idealizing selfobject transference was reduced. It can also be stated that as a result of the bit-by-bit disillusionment, the structure-building process of transmuting internalization was concurrently set into motion. Ms. O.'s idealizing selfobject needs underwent significant change. I was no longer held up as the omniscient selfobject with the final word in understanding human behavior. Rather, I was appreciated as someone who was understanding, knowledgeable, and helpful, but who had limitations. For example, she wondered if there could be other modalities of treatment that could take less time in achieving the same success. It could be stated that in ego-psychological terms her view of me was more mature and realistic. It was at this point, approximately two and a half years after the beginning of treatment, that a stable secondary mirror transference emerged (in the narrower sense). More and more she had been able to recognize and implement her considerable abilities and talents. Her advancement at work continued. She became the manager of her department and then took a higher-paying managerial position with a competing store. During this time she was able to make demands on her husband to share in household responsibilities. Not infrequently her demands led to heated arguments. In general, however, she was able to take a stand, and they arrived at satisfactory compromises that allowed for an increase in mutually shared activities. For example, Ms. O. had become popular at work with a number of administrators who invited her and her husband to several social gatherings.

HER MARITAL RELATIONSHIP

It became clearer that her choice of husband was based to a great extent on her primitive idealization – subservience to the powerful godlike rescuer.* For example, Ms. O.'s husband was a successful real estate broker and respected community leader who served on a number of executive boards of charitable organizations. She had initially met him at a community fund-raising event at which he was the main speaker. Ms. O. described her feelings of "being in a trance" after she was introduced to him by a friend. She found herself following him around throughout the evening as he spoke with the many people who introduced themselves to him after his speech. She was attracted to his impressive and imposing appearance. He was older than she – a tall, slightly grey-haired Hispanic man who had a "booming" voice that commanded everyone's attention. When he became aware of her interest in him, he asked her out and began dating her until they were married four months later. Ms. O. reported that she knew very little about her husband during the time of

---

*Archaic forms of idealized selfobjects are experienced similarly by patients no matter what the patients' socioeconomic and cultural life circumstances. The experience is dutifulness to a godlike image or force which can provide a neverending wellspring of relief and happiness. This sense of a boundless and constantly unfolding wellspring of comfort is a major aspect of the experience. The archaic grandiose self is also experienced similarly by various kinds of patients in that it is a boundless and constantly unfolding experience of power and strength.

their courtship as she had asked few questions out of fear of upsetting him. She thought that if he wished her to know more about him, he would tell her. Only after they were married did she learn that he had been previously married for a short while five years earlier, and had a 4-year-old son who was living out of the country with his mother.

Ms. O. described her "trance" feeling as persisting during the first year of her marriage. She was 23 and had just moved to the United States when she met her husband, and she was living in a single small room while working as a waitress. When she was married she moved into her husband's large luxury apartment which had a doorman and a swimming pool. It was during the second year of marriage that Ms. O. sought treatment, after she had begun to suffer severe anxiety and a variety of physical symptoms as her feelings of worthlessness intensified within the marriage.

Ms. O.'s evolving and changing demands for her husband to recognize her in a different way, and to cooperate in making compromises in their lives, was initially surprising to him and resulted in angry exchanges that characterized much of their relationship during this time.

A major difference was Ms. O.'s changing attitude about sexuality. Initially she had believed that it was her role as a "good wife" always to be available sexually to her husband, as her mother was to her father. Her fantasies during intercourse were elaborations on earlier masturbatory fantasies in which she would submit sexually to a powerful male figure who rescued her. She could reach orgasm only when she called up these fantasies. She frequently was left unsatisfied as she dared not make sexual demands on her husband. She would then masturbate after waiting for her husband to fall asleep.

Ms. O. described herself as "unable to do without" her submission fantasies. She recalled occasionally masturbating with these fantasies when she was single, but the frequency increased after she was married. We came to understand the increased frequency as directly connected to her growing feelings of worthlessness, which had intensified in her marriage. Masturbation provided her with some of the stimulation that was much needed to maintain her self-cohesiveness.

As treatment progressed and as Ms. O. gained a firmer sense of self, her masturbation diminished significantly. The quality of her sexual experience also changed. She no longer relied upon submission fantasies to reach orgasm. Rather, she began to develop a freedom and spontaneity in the sexual act, wherein her concentration was more upon the mutuality of the lovemaking experience and less upon herself. Initially, she was concerned about the resulting loss of her erotic intensity and tended to compare her newfound freedom as inferior. She wondered if she was losing her sexuality.

Ms. O.'s reaction is characteristic of severely damaged patients who require intense erotic stimulation to shore up an enfeebled self. The diminishing of erotic intensity as a result of accruing self structure inevitably leads these patients to compare the new experience unfavorably with the old, thus interfering with the appreciation and enjoyment of the new and different experience. Frequently these patients will complain that they have "fallen out of love" because they have equated the intensity of the eroticism with being in love and having "good sex." This equation is a rationalization motivated not only by psychological needs but also reinforced by commonly held cultural attitudes.

As Ms. O. was able to experience greater freedom and was able to place greater demands on her husband, she worked through this initial feeling of loss of the erotic intensity and became able to give recognition to what she described as "a fuller, more joyful sexual experience." It is important to note that Ms. O. was beginning to experience a balance and mix of various affective states, which included a level of eroticism. It might be suggested here, and is also illustrated later in the case of Mr. V., that the degree of the erotic intensity of a sexual act is in direct proportion to the severity of the threat to self-cohesion.

This can be observed in pornography where the sought-after intensity and stimulation require that one or the other of the partners be psychologically demeaned or physically threatened in a variety of ways, such as through various devices of torture.

The admixture of eroticism in healthy sexuality requires further study. The question can be asked: Is sexual attraction possible without some conscious or unconscious threat to one's self-esteem? That is, can there be sexual attraction without at least some concern about potential rejection, whether real or imagined?

By the conclusion of Ms. O.'s treatment, she was no longer preoccupied with the possibility of her husband leaving if she did not accede to his sexual demands. Her sense of worth and desirability had developed and with it her acknowledgment of her own overall attractiveness as a woman. Contrary to the way she had felt earlier, Ms. O. was now confident that she could meet other men and possibly remarry if her husband left.

This is not to say that Ms. O. was not fearful during those times she expressed her needs to her husband. Earlier fears of being destroyed and abandoned reemerged during these inter-changes. At first, she was certain that her husband would "throw her out on the street" or leave her for another woman. She also feared that I would likewise disapprove of her assertiveness and would "throw her out" of treatment.

She was surprised that her marriage continued throughout the many discussions with her husband. She was delighted that in time he was able to consider and understand what was important to her, and that he could make compromises including giving attention to her individual sexual needs. In time, her husband also agreed to her wish to have a child. She gave birth to a baby boy approximately two years before finishing treatment, which was concluded after approximately seven years.

TERMINATION

At the start of the seventh year and within the context of this general improvement in her life—her work, relationship, and family—Ms. O. expressed a wish to conclude her treatment. As her wish was explored, she expressed excitement over her accomplishments in treatment as well as her hopes and aspirations for the future. At this point, she was secure about what she had gained in our work and excited about the prospect of facing life without treatment. As we explored further, she was aware that termination of treatment, though the prospect was exciting, contained elements of sadness and tearfulness. Her tearfulness prevailed even more when an actual termination date was set for approximately six months later.

It was during this time that there was a revival of the self-doubts of "being driven back" into her old feelings of submission. These were accompanied by a number of traveling dreams, in some of which she would be leading groups of people. These dreams were accompanied by considerable anxiety, which occasionally caused her to awaken. The dreams were understood to represent both conscious and unconscious fears of going ahead with her life, of facing separation, and they included components of "being destroyed." Another aspect of the dreams was that her moving ahead represented not only the loss of me and the analysis, but also of her husband and son. A major theme here was the residue of her fear that she would be abandoned and left alone if she continued her "travels" and her going forward in life.

In the latter half of her final year of treatment, she made

plans for more frequent visits to her mother and father. Up until this time, although the family had visited when her son was born, there had been no plans for further visits. Ms. O. hoped that she could build on some of the positive qualities of her family, which she had recovered during the treatment.

Four years after the conclusion of treatment, I received a graduation announcement from her with an enclosed note that all was going well. She was especially proud that her son had entered the first grade.

As previously noted, Kohut (1977, p. 4) taught that termination of treatment with the narcissistic personality disorder has been reached when one or both of two treatment tasks has been completed: first, the primary defect in the self has been exposed, and by way of the working-through process and the process of transmuting internalization, new reliable structures have been acquired; and second, the patient has come to an understanding and mastery of the defenses surrounding the primary defect in the self, in regard to the formation of compensatory structures and in terms of the relationship of the compensatory structures to the primary defect.

Ms. O. was able to accomplish both of these treatment tasks. It was clear that she had suffered primary structural defects in both the exhibitionistic and idealizing poles of the self. She was able to explore in considerable detail the childhood traumas which had created fixations on primitive configurations of the grandiose self and idealized parental image. She was able to get in touch with her primitive fears of destroying and being destroyed, as well as her childhood disillusionments with both parents.

As treatment proceeded, she was able to work through her fears of catastrophic destruction and began to risk gradual exhibitionistic expressions of assertiveness and needs for mirroring both in the treatment and social settings. Her many physical symptoms, which could be viewed as defensive reactions against her feelings of emptiness and the deadening experience of worth-lessness, subsided completely.

These developmental changes attest to the accruing of structure in the exhibitionistic sector of the supraordinate self. These acquired structures can be considered to be reliable; for example, Ms. O.'s abilities to pursue and to implement her goals in treatment and in her life situation were not only successful but lasting (as indicated by her graduation announcement and note to me.)

Ms. O. was able to analyze the defensive relationship between her idealization of the powerful and all-wise selfobject figure and her enfeebled grandiose self. She explored in detail the factors leading to a fixation on her primitive form of idealization, and understood it as compensatory for the severely thwarted development of her grandiose self. The idealizing selfobject transference evolved in treatment from its initial archaic form, when Ms. O. had looked helplessly and submissively to the selfobject analyst for her thoughts, ideals, and values, to the development of her own stable personal values and ideals encompassing learning, understanding, and caring for individuals and the society.

In reconstructing the interferences as well as the positives in Ms. O.'s development, we can more fully understand her potential for growth in the treatment and especially her childhood reliance on subservient idealization to maintain stability. Ms. O. learned from her family that she had been a contented baby during her first two years, when she was breast-fed and slept with her mother. It is likely that Ms. O. had experienced caring and warmth and that her very early mirroring and idealizing needs were met. However, she began to suffer massive deprivation when she was taken from her mother's bed and left to cry unattended night after night. Throughout her childhood and adolescence, she had been rejected in her attempts to formulate and express her ideas and thoughts. Her developing grandiose self and needs for mirroring were severely thwarted. Major structural damage can be seen as occurring in this sector of the self.

Whereas Ms. O. also suffered early traumatic disillusionment with her parents and older brother as idealized selfobjects, her traumas in this area of her self development seemed less severe than those suffered in the establishment of the grandiose self. For example, Ms. O. was able to recover significant idealizing experiences with her mother, father, brother, and aunt. Although Ms. O. remained fixed on an archaic idealized selfobject configuration, it was through this fixation that she was able to maintain a selfobject relatedness (albeit subservient) and a self-cohesiveness (albeit fragile). Ms. O.'s primitive idealized selfobject configuration served to make up for, although in a limited way, the weakness in the pole of the grandiose self.

She turned to her aunt as the only person whom she felt could protect her from her brother's sexual abuse. At the same time, however, she could not speak about her terror at hearing her mother and father engaging in sexual intercourse. Her aunt, as did her mother and father, failed her as an idealized selfobject who could understand the extent of her fears. Through treatment she was able to recover the thwarted idealizing experiences that were integral in her movement away from her fixation on an archaic form of idealization to a different level of idealizing selfobject transference. Treatment also enabled her to move ahead in her overall development and realize important nuclear ambitions and ideals.

Kohut (1977, 1984) has emphasized that termination is a process stage of treatment that evolves naturally, without the patient being pushed to consider termination and without the setting of fixed dates for ending. Kohut has taught us to trust the patient's wish to terminate, especially when the desire to conclude is not sudden or urgent, but, as with Ms. O., comes about after years of work. The analyst should be able to formulate the patient's progress in dynamic and structural terms to determine whether there has been sufficient development which would make further analysis unnecessary. Also, it is important that at the time of termination the patient has been able to move toward the establishment of a variety of reliable selfobjects outside the analytic situation, as was true with Ms. O. in her academic, social, and professional pursuits. For example, as Ms. O. was able to appreciate an ever-expanding scope of learning, she formed idealizing selfobject ties with a number of college instructors who were encouraging and supportive of her learning. She sought out and found understanding and empathic colleagues who not only served as like-minded twinship selfobjects who were pursuing similar academic interests, but were admiring and mirroring selfobjects as well. Her husband, also, was able to come to a greater appreciation of her goals and successes.

Both Ms. O. and her husband had looked happily toward the birth of their child. She enthusiastically described the "natural childbirth" delivery in which her husband participated, as well as the initial moment-to-moment experiences in caring for her son. Ms. O. was impressed with and proud of the day-by-day development she observed in her child. It was clear that she felt a freedom and joy in her mirroring of his budding grandiosity, and in allowing for early idealizing merger states especially during breast-feeding.

Even though it was concluded upon reconstruction that Ms. O. had experienced similar nurturing experiences during the first two years of her life, and that she had desired to have a child from the beginning of her marriage, it can be assumed that without treatment she would not have been able freely, spontaneously, and without anxiety to enjoy and give deeply to her child. The intense fears which had prevented her from asserting her wishes and realizing her hopes would have undoubtedly interfered.

CHAPTER 16

Treatment of a Borderline Personality Disorder: The Case of Mr. V.

The following is an example of treatment with a patient with a borderline personality organization. Before getting into the case, we would like to discuss briefly the diagnosis of "borderline."

The concept of "borderline" has been given considerable attention in the literature. Knight (1953) in his seminal paper, "Borderline States," questions the validity of the use of "borderline state" as a diagnostic term for those patients who fall between the neurotic – or relatively healthy – end of the spectrum of problems, and the psychotic. Knight thought that a much more precise diagnosis should be made that identifies the particular type of pathology. Kernberg (1968, 1971, 1975), perhaps more than any other theorist, has attempted to sharpen our understanding of this disorder. He considered the term "borderline personality organization" rather than "borderline states" or other terms to describe more accurately this particular population of patients (1975, pp. 3–4). Kernberg considers these patients to have a stable, though pathological, personality. The following are some of the characteristics that Kernberg has found "borderlines" to have in common: (1) diffuse anxiety; (2) ego weaknesses such as lack of impulse control, lack of anxiety tolerance, shift to primitive and illogical thinking, use of primitive defenses such as projective identification (attributing one's own thoughts, ideas, and feelings to another and then identifying with these projected thoughts, ideas, and feelings), denial, devaluation, omnipotence, primitive idealization, splitting (keeping apart introjections or identifications of opposite qualities, which results in experiencing self and others as all good or all bad); (3) pathology of internalized object relationships, which primarily results from the ego's incapacity for synthesizing the "good" and "bad" introjections and identifications; and (4) excessive pregenital and oral aggression that, through the defensive process of projection, distorts the object (or aspects of the object) as dangerous. Splitting then becomes necessary to preserve the internalized good objects from the internalized dangerous ("all bad") objects. Therefore, according to Kernberg, excessive pregenital and oral aggression is a major causative condition that promotes splitting and pathological internal object relationships.

As stated earlier, Kohut (1984) defined the borderline personality as a covert psychotic personality but one with developed defensive structures. While Kohut was aware that his experience with "borderlines" was limited, he concluded that treatment of borderline and psychotic personalities must be modified because of the severity of the traumas suffered by these individuals and the lack of the development of a firm and cohesive self. It is therefore doubtful that – due to their chaotic childhood selfobject experiences – these patients could tolerate the usual in-depth analytic exploration and loosening of defenses. Speaking about his own experience in working with the "borderline patient," Kohut wondered about his own limitations in being able to maintain a reliable empathic bond when the patient ". . . would have to tolerate protracted experience of prepsychological chaos and . . . borrow the analyst's personality organization in order to survive" (p. 9). Kohut's honesty is helpful in alerting us to the difficulty in attempting to maintain an empathic immersion into the inner life of these patients. In-depth psychoanalysis may not be feasible with most borderline patients. However, Kohut suggests that these patients may evolve into analyzable narcissistic personalities if the analyst can persist in maintaining the empathic experience-near treatment focus.

The following treatment sessions illustrate the primitiveness and chaotic quality of the childhood selfobject experience of my "borderline" patient. Also illustrated are my efforts to maintain the empathic stance in the face of his explosiveness and extreme vulnerability, and the step-by-step process which led to his acquiring reliable compensatory structure, and then to a successful completion of treatment. As with Ms. O., I have attempted to reveal as accurately as possible my moment-to-moment thoughts and feelings as well as those of my patient. Also, I have again included a discussion of the self psychology theory as it applies to my patient's behavior and the treatment process.

REFERRAL INFORMATION

Mr. V. was referred by a colleague who was seeing a distant cousin of his in psychoanalysis. Mr. V.'s cousin requested a referral from my colleague as he wished to "persuade" Mr. V. to enter treatment. The cousin considered Mr. V. to be a wanderer and a "wasted genius" who did not know what direction to take in life in order to fulfill his many talents. My colleague did not have any further information about Mr. V. It was understood that he would give his patient my name as a referral and that Mr. V. would then arrange the appointment.

TELEPHONE CONTACT

Mr. V. telephoned me for an appointment. In a matter-of-fact way he introduced himself and asked: "When could I see you?" Whereas it goes without saying that empathic immersion by way of the telephone is highly limited, I was able to get a general sense of coldness and indifference in his tone. I was aware of feeling confused about his wishing to make an appointment. It was as if it mattered very little to him whether or not I would be able to arrange a time. However, due to the limitations of communicating by telephone, I was not able to get an accurate impression of what Mr. V. was experiencing and I therefore, was unable to determine what was in ascendancy. Having inadequate understanding, I was left with my own confusion. I therefore made no attempt to offer my thoughts about his apparent disinterest in making an appointment. I simply offered him an available time for a consultation, which he accepted in a similarly disinterested way. I told him my address after which he said "O.K.," and then hung up the phone without further comment.

This brief sequence highlights the initial understanding of a patient that usually begins on the telephone. It is, therefore, useful to be aware of the difficulties. For example, while I was able to gain some general sense of Mr. V.'s experience, empathic immersion was necessarily limited by way of the telephone. (It can be suggested that even after lengthy treatment in which an empathic selfobject bond has been established, telephone discussions can be seriously disruptive to the treatment by limiting the potential for empathic immersion.)

Having limited access to Mr. V.'s experience I was, therefore, limited in my understanding at that point. I was left not knowing what Mr. V.'s seeming disinterest was all about. It was important that I was aware of my confusion. Being in touch with my response alerted me to the fact that I was as of yet not in touch with the fullness of his experience.

My awareness that I was not clear about the meaning of Mr. V.'s indifference gave me an opportunity to begin the process of understanding the "why" of my confusion. If I had not been in touch with what was going on inside me, I would have reacted without the benefit of this awareness. I might therefore have risked unconscious gratification of my own needs; in other words, I might have imposed countertransference selfobject needs on the patient. For example, it is conceivable that, in an effort to relieve my uncomfortable feeling of not knowing if Mr. V. was interested in making an appointment, I might have questioned him about his wish to see me or I might have in some way said something to relieve my discomfort. In any case, my responses would have been serving my own needs and would not have furthered my understanding of Mr. V.

INITIAL SESSION

Mr. V. was twenty minutes early for his session. When I opened the hallway door he said without hesitation, "You're the guy I spoke to." Then, without waiting for a reply, "Well, I'm here. You're ready, aren't you? Let's get this thing over with." He started moving toward my office door.

I felt a sudden wave of anxiety; I had the impression that this man would not hesitate to open my office door and intrude on the patient I was seeing and who was waiting for me to return. For a brief moment I was torn between making an attempt to be attuned to what was going on with Mr. V., and my impulse to somehow stop him from opening the door to my consulting room. I envisioned my patient, who was waiting, becoming extremely frightened should Mr. V. enter. Again I was left with confusion as to the meaning of his behavior. However, unlike the telephone conversation, during which I had attempted to remain focused only on understanding Mr. V., I was forced in this situation to consider the welfare of the patient behind my office door. Also, unlike the way I had felt during the telephone conversation, I was experiencing considerable anxiety mixed with reactive annoyance at Mr. V.'s intrusiveness.

My dilemma here was setting limits with Mr. V. while still preserving the potential for establishing an empathic treatment bond. I was aware that even though I was anxious and annoyed, I could begin to understand Mr. V. only if I remained connected to his experience. As these thoughts flashed through my mind, I was also aware of how relieving it would be to forego my attempts to understand Mr. V. and express my evoked annoyance by demanding that he not enter my consulting room – or, perhaps, to physically block him by standing in front of the door. I was reminded of my previous traditional psychoanalytic training, which legitimized my controlling Mr. V. from an experience-distant perspective. Theories based on the concepts of drives, and/or theories that focus on the evaluation of the various functions of the mind as they relate to the strengths of the drives, justify an understanding of the patient through his or her behavior or actions rather than what he or she is experiencing. For instance, the analyst might evaluate Mr. V. as having poor impulse control and poor reality testing, based on his speaking to me and moving toward my consultation room in such a manner.

The same analyst might view Mr. V.'s behavior in terms of impulsive and aggressive acting out against some form of "bad" self or object representation projected onto the analyst. Within this theoretical context the analyst may well understand his or her own reactions as being provoked by the patient's attempt to extract retribution, albeit through projections. Based upon this theoretical understanding, one can easily see how the analyst would feel justified in controlling Mr. V., much as I had wished to do in my fleeting fantasy. For example, the analyst, in an effort to help the patient control such impulsivity and correct such faulty reality testing, might demand that Mr. V. stop moving toward the door, that he take a seat, and so on. Since Mr. V.'s actions would likely be understood as a provocation, the analyst might then confront him about his misplaced aggression. For example, this might be done through a questioning nod of the head, a frown, or a tone of voice that would clearly indicate that his actions were inappropriate. On the other hand, the therapist might become openly angry as a way of emphasizing the seriousness of Mr. V.'s actions and helping him to acknowledge his pathology.

Returning to my dilemma of stopping Mr. V. from entering my consulting room while also establishing an empathic connection, I attempted to keep in mind my annoyance, anxiety, and confusion while as much as possible immersing myself in Mr. V.'s experience.

As Mr. V. came slowly toward me, I sensed that he was calm and somewhat preoccupied, as if he were worried or depressed. As I began to pick up his affective tone, he became much less threatening, which greatly modified my first impression of him as a potentially destructive intruder. My effort to "place myself in the patient's shoes" led me to question my assumption that he was intent on being disruptive.

However, as he moved past me and toward my consultation room, I felt a second wave of anxiety. At that point I gave up my effort at trying empathically to understand and returned to my initial view of him as deliberately intrusive.

As he passed by me I said sharply, "Excuse me! We have about twenty minutes before our appointment. You can sit here, and I'll come out again when it's time." Mr. V. seemed stunned. Without saying anything, he stood motionless for a moment; then he turned away from me, walked to the other side of the waiting area, and took a seat.

As I returned to my waiting patient, I was concerned about how easily I had removed myself from Mr. V.'s experience and responded to him as if I were an outside observer. My rising anxiety over protecting my patient, coupled with my previous traditional training, had led me to exerting control over Mr. V. without regard for his experience. Upon reconsideration I thought my intervention had been unnecessary. Although I had succeeded in stopping Mr. V. from moving further toward my inner office, I could have accomplished this by remaining in his experience and communicating my understanding (even though limited) from that vantage point. I thought that I could have related to him my sense that he was preoccupied, worried, and perhaps inattentive to his actions. An empathic communication of my understanding thus far might have been: "I know you would like to get started, but I am with someone else right now. I'll be out in twenty minutes." In this way I would have communicated a general understanding of his experience of being focused only on beginning the consultation, without consideration of the arranged time or any of the usual social amenities that accompany meeting someone for the first time. It was his experience of wanting to get started that, after reconsideration, I thought to be in ascendancy and therefore a recognizable experience for Mr. V.

As stated earlier, **empathy is an intersubjective process consisting of the therapist's immersion into the patient's experience, which continuously shifts and accrues new qualities and coloration as the patient's experiences are being understood. Therefore, the analyst's experience of the patient shifts and changes in resonance with the patient's fluctuating experiences of the analyst.** Intersubjectivity as defined here is not only the opening of two differently organized subjective worlds to each other (Atwood and Stolorow 1984, Stolorow et al. 1987); rather it is a process that requires an active immersion and expanding attunement on the part of the analyst. The patient, of course, responds to the therapist's empathy without any requirement to understand the experience of the analyst.

In reflecting further about what I might have said to Mr. V. in those opening moments, the question might be asked why I would not immediately clarify the correct time of his appointment. After all, it might have been unclear to him. Perhaps I had inadvertently given him an earlier time, and he thought he was being considerate of me by moving toward my office door with the idea of getting started without further delay. Would not a simple inquiry into his understanding of the time set for his appointment have been the first step in coming to a diagnostic understanding, whatever the analyst's theoretical persuasion? Certainly, if I had learned through my experience-distant questioning that he thought he was late and therefore wished to get started, my evaluation as well as my intervention would have necessarily been different. I might have then viewed Mr. V. as highly motivated to begin treatment rather than considering him deliberately intrusive.

But what about my rethinking of my initial intervention within the theoretical context of self psychology? Would I not be making a similar error by not questioning Mr. V.?

These "what if" questions can only be answered by specu-
lation, and are therefore limited in value. However, they are
necessary if we are to further our learning from our errors as well
as our successes.

The creation of a breach in the empathic bond through
direct questioning of the patient has been discussed earlier, with
regard to Ms. O. It was emphasized that direct questioning may
be necessary, especially when there is an immediate need to
know certain information such as suicidal or homicidal intentions. Disruptions which usually occur, however, can be kept to
a minimum if the therapist's questions arise from the patient's
experience, as illustrated in my work with my depressed patient,
Ms. P. (see Chapter 13).

With these thoughts in mind, I can answer "no" to the
inquiry whether or not I would be risking misunderstanding Mr.
V. by focusing on his experience rather than clarifying his
appointment time. To take it a step further, it can be suggested
that focusing on Mr. V.'s experience is the only avenue to
beginning to understand the dynamics of his behavior. In re-
viewing the initial moments, I came to understand that Mr. V.'s
experience in ascendancy was his desire to get started. Therefore,
any direct questioning of his awareness of the time of his appointment, though it might temporarily be relieving to me,
would likely be outside of his experience and thus not helpful in
understanding him from the experience-near vantage point. As
stated, questions that do not arise from the patient's experience
and do not serve to further the understanding of what the patient
is experiencing, inevitably interfere with the developing selfobject bond. Direct questioning can be viewed as a tool of *introspection* when it furthers experience-near understanding of the patient's experience; direct questioning can be viewed as a tool of
extrospection when it furthers experience-distant observation.

After finishing the session with my previous patient, I looked for Mr. V., but he was not in the waiting area. Just then I saw him turning the corner of the office hallway and coming toward me. Without blinking he stared at me and said loudly, "I tried to find your bathroom. You told me to sit so I thought I might as well sit on the toilet." Mr. V. moved quickly past me as he was talking and toward my office door, which I had left open. He walked in while I was still in the waiting area.

My thoughts flashed to the possibility that he might turn to me and invite me into my own office. I was aware that I was becoming annoyed just as I had when I first met him. This time, however, I was not experiencing anxiety. I was also aware that I was having some difficulty in immersing myself in his experience. Whereas I had wanted very much to understand Ms. O., I now sensed that I did not want to try to understand Mr. V. I was even feeling some dislike for him, which, however, diminished quickly when I connected my experience of Mr. V. to several personal past traumas in which I had suffered such things as being rejected and being taken for granted. In a single moment I was able to call upon my years of personal analysis to help me identify telescoped derivatives of past traumas (countertransference), which were triggered by Mr. V.'s seeming disregard.

PERSONAL ANALYSIS

The importance of personal analysis as part of the psychoanalyst's training is well known and is a requirement in psychoanalytic training institutes throughout the world. Kohut has repeatedly emphasized the importance of recognizing clues to countertransference responses, which normally occur when working with narcissistically damaged patients.

The analyst's own narcissistic needs for recognition and acknowledgment may make it difficult for him or her to tolerate the patient's demands for mirroring mobilized infantile narcissism, and for allowing twinship and merger selfobject transferences to develop. The analyst may, for example, become impatient or annoyed at the patient's emerging grandiosity and thereby fail to recognize the importance of the developing mirror transference. In subtle or maybe not-so-subtle ways, the analyst is likely to communicate his or her negative reactions. It is not uncommon for an analyst – as in the case with Mr. V. – to justify these reactions theoretically by interventions directed at curbing the patient's exhibitionism. Kohut (1971) points out that the patient's twinship and merger needs may trigger the analyst's boredom, resulting in a lack of attention and a general lack of interest and involvement in his or her patient.

The idealizing needs of the patient can also present countertransference problems for the analyst. Residues of problems that the analyst might have suffered in his or her own development of satisfactory idealized selfobjects might be triggered by the patient's overt admiration. As previously discussed, the analyst may attempt to ward off his or her discomfort by correcting the patient's overestimation, and thereby seriously interfere with the developing idealization.

Such responses are only some of what can be considered "clues" to countertransference phenomena. Clues offer opportunities to explore unanalyzed residues of the analyst's own past traumas that have interfered with the fully successful internalizations of the selfobject functions provided in his or her own analysis. The self-analytic exploration of these clues, which is commonly referred to as "self analysis," should be helpful in diminishing the interfering responses. If this self-analytic process is not helpful and interferences persist, it goes without saying that the analyst should consider returning to analysis at least for a period of time, to complete the working-through process of those residues of traumas that have obviously interfered with transmuting internalization of needed selfobject functions and the development of sufficient self structure. By this recommendation we are also stating that the analyst has the responsibility to have worked through the effects of past traumas, and to have developed adequate self structure, so that he or she can allow for and tolerate the continued unfolding of the patient's selfobject demands and thereby make the analytic process possible. While we are emphasizing the responsibility of the analyst to undergo analysis and possibly re-analysis, we are not suggesting that there is any such thing as a perfect analysis that holds out the promise of meeting perfectionistic analytic goals. Kohut warned against such perfectionistic strivings. An analysis can be considered to have achieved satisfactory results if it enables one to maintain a creative life of well-being and inner balance, and to successfully utilize self-analysis when under stress, according to Kohut (1984, p. 154).

After my brief moment of self-analysis I was able to turn my attention to what Mr. V. was experiencing.

He walked to the cushioned chair in the middle of the room and dropped into it. There was a loud crack. He said, "I'll sit here in this big green one."

I immediately became concerned about my chair, which I had just purchased. I was sure that it was broken. My thoughts flashed to where I had put the sales slip – maybe it could be repaired. As I became aware that I had been more concerned with my chair than with understanding Mr. V., he slid his body down on the seat and accidentally knocked over a small table with his outstretched legs.

He sat suddenly upright. "Oops, does this thing break?" He lifted the table above his head and then set it down. "I guess not. When I knock it over again, I won't have to worry about it breaking. Well, let's start – let's see."

As Mr. V. was speaking, I felt a strong urge to smile. I was no longer annoyed, anxious, or feeling dislike for Mr. V. There was something comical about the situation. Mr. V. had not only nearly walked in on my patient, but had unhesitatingly made his way into my office, chosen a chair that he liked and then managed to break it, turned over a table, and was now directing me to begin the session. I thought once again how easy it would be to evaluate Mr. V.'s behavior as an outside observer and in extrospective theoretical terms. For example, within this context Mr. V.'s breaking the chair and turning over and then lifting the table could be seen as a breakthrough of aggressive impulses resulting from poor ego controls. After further evaluation Mr. V.'s behavior might be viewed as resentful attempts motivated by envy and directed to destroying projected internalized "bad objects." How relieving it would be to bypass the empathic experience-near process of understanding and conclude that Mr. V. was out to do damage. I could then with theoretical assuredness confront Mr. V. with his destructive purpose, and thereby exert control over his "disturbing" behavior.

My humorous feelings and random thoughts were responses to my extrospective observation of Mr. V. This indicated to me that I was for the most part outside of his experience. Realizing this, I was able to shift from the experience-distant mode of observation (and response) to placing myself in Mr. V.'s experience. As I refocused my attention upon capturing Mr. V.'s experience, I was able to get a clearer and more defined impression of his physical characteristics. For example, in the first moments of meeting Mr. V. as an outside observer, I saw him as slim, tall, muscular, athletic-looking, and in general a strong and forceful person. His chiseled facial features and short haircut added to my picture of him as "tough." However, as I began to tune in to Mr. V.'s experience in a more consistent manner I began to get a radically different impression.

After Mr. V. set the table back onto the floor and began to speak I sensed that he was anxious. Rather than being forceful, athletic, strong, and "tough," he seemed vulnerable and unsure. There was an almost imperceptible twisting and thrusting of his whole body. He pressed his hand against one side of his face and then the other. For a moment he would rest his chin on the palm of his hand and then suddenly snap his head slightly backward. He shifted his weight from side to side and at times leaned forward, crossing his legs. I sensed that he was maintaining a continuous flow of movement at an unchanging level of intensity.

Mr. V. continued, "Let's see, let's see–hmmm. Yes, I know where we can start–hmmm, yes, I know exactly where to start–hmmm–I don't want to be here–hmmm–Robert [Mr. V.'s cousin] said if I did not get my act together–I would have to leave–"

At this point he suddenly sat up and began to speak loudly–almost shouting. "He gave me a deadline of two months for me to get work." Mr. V. was becoming more and more intense. "You see I came here six months ago from California to get work–hmmm–Robert was supposed to put me up for a week until I found work–it got stretched out for six months and now he wants me out. Hmmm."

Mr. V. continued speaking in a nonstop manner about his visit with Robert and his feeling of "being pushed" into treatment. Throughout, he continued humming when there was a pause in his thinking as if, with his continuous movements and sounds, he was attempting to maintain a certain level of intensity. While Mr. V. looked directly at me and spoke directly to me, I sensed that his concentration was elsewhere. He seemed to be reciting some soliloquy in his own personal world. I began to feel strangely alone, like an unwanted anonymous observer.

It should be emphasized that, as with all experiences, my experience of Mr. V.'s experience was continually expanding and evolving through my attunement to his evolving experience of my response to him. As previously discussed, this "feedback loop" is how we define the intersubjective process.

The reader may ask the question: What about your experience-near response to Mr. V.'s unfolding experience – could not that feeling of being anonymous and excluded be countertransference responses, in the same way your feeling of dislike was a countertransference response to Mr. V.'s behavior from an experience-distant perspective? The answer is yes, it could well be. Interfering residues of the analyst's traumatic past experiences can be triggered by being "in the patient's shoes" as well as being outside of them. It can be suggested that such residues are more likely to be triggered from prolonged immersion into the patient's deepest levels of emotional life. Self-analysis (employing the self-analytic function) is a must to diminish interferences which prevent continuous immersion into the patient's experience.

To further answer the question, my feeling of being excluded, while triggering past traumas, was not intense and therefore did not interfere with my staying with Mr. V.'s experience.

Therefore, I was able tentatively to begin to understand – which is the first of the two steps of treatment, the second being explaining – that Mr. V. was in a powerful emotional state of grandiosity. He was in his own world from which I was excluded. This suggested that his grandiosity was defensively reactive to a threat to the self and was an effort to maintain self cohesion. As previously noted, Kohut has described this reaction in dynamic and economic terms as the *hypercathexis* of the grandiose self.

Through his humming and his continuous movement, Mr. V. maintained an uninterrupted flow of sensations. As part of my first theoretical impression, I saw this as providing him with a continuous feeling of wholeness and cohesiveness which protected him from experiencing potential self-threatening intrusions by me. If my tentative formulations were accurate, it would follow that Mr. V. suffered nuclear defects in the self, and that his manifestations of grandiosity were reactively defensive (defensive structure) in that they functioned only to cover over these defects rather than reliably compensating for them (compensatory structure).

These theoretical considerations, which were formulated from experience-near information gathering, contrast dramatically with those that are based on experience-distant observations. Simply put: Mr. V.'s powerful and controlling behavior, and his continuous talking and movement, constituted an effort to sustain an enfeebled self by creating an impregnable wall of sensation through which no one could intrude. This conceptualization is obviously different from that in which Mr. V. is depicted as someone motivated by revenge and envy, and consciously or unconsciously intent on some form of symbolic destruction. It is also apparent that because the understanding of him was different, the treatment interventions would necessarily be different as well.

Although my formulations were necessarily tentative, empathic immersion into Mr. V.'s experience in these first moments had provided me with a beginning understanding that would be revised partially or completely depending on further information gained through expanding attunement.

After speaking for some time about the details of his visit and about his feeling that his cousin was pressuring him by giving him a deadline to move out, Mr. V. suddenly jerked forward in his seat. He then visibly tensed his body, leaned back, and tightly gripped the arms of the chair. I got the impression that he was extremely anxious and was bracing himself as though he were expecting some kind of assault.

He was quiet for several seconds, then hesitatingly and quietly asked: "What's your fee?"

For the first time I sensed that he wished a response from me. I understood this as his risking an emotional shift away from

his powerful protective grandiose expressions and allowing himself a tenuous moment of relatedness to me. Before I could
answer him, Mr. V. abruptly stood up, moved around the chair,
and then dropped down stiffly onto one of the chair's arms.

"Robert got me into this. There is no way I am going to pay for this.
People should not have to pay to get treatment – (Hmmm). The system
is no good. I pay taxes. I made a hundred thousand dollars last year
selling computers. I won three national awards. I was a national
salesman. I had no territorial limits. My area was the whole country. I
paid my share of taxes." Mr. V. again abruptly stood up and began
circling the chair. "Take, take, take, everyone wants to suck you dry.
My wife took every dime. Thank God I don't have any children. The
divorce judge would have given them to her. Why not, she got the
house and the car." He paused and was silent. He seemed relaxed, sad,
and deep in thought.

In my attempt to capture Mr. V.'s experience as fully as
possible (expanding attunement) I once again sensed that there
was a sudden heightening of his grandiosity at the point when he
wished a response from me. This seemed to be further evidence
supporting my initial tentative postulation that Mr. V. suffered
structural deficiencies in the nuclear self, which were covered
over at times of vulnerability through defensive activation of
grandiose self configurations. My expanding attunement also
allowed me to perceive at times what seemed to be a quality of
intense thoughtfulness, of which I had not been aware in the
opening moments of our session. Even though Mr. V. seemed to
be in his own grandiose world and quite fearful of any response
from me, I thought he might be able to accept my understanding
of what he was experiencing with regard to his divorce, which
seemed clearly in ascendancy.

I said, "It's like everything was taken from you." He stopped his circling and turned directly to me. "That's right," he responded. "I was ripped off like I have always been ripped off." He remained. "So how are you going to rip me off? I'm curious to see if you're going to take my money like all the rest. I've read about therapists. How many times are you going to ask me to come? More times more money, huh?"

Mr. V. was able to accept my understanding and felt free to reveal his expectations and curiosity about me: I, like everyone else, would probably try to rip him off. This seemed to be a favorable prognostic sign, in that his capacity to accept my intervention and to reveal further thoughts indicated at least some potential for taking in and making use of my functions as an empathic selfobject.

Again, I wished to communicate my understanding and include in my communication the recognition of his ability to reveal specifics of his expectations of me. It is suggested that this recognition, with its validating and confirming effects, facilitates the internalization of the empathic functions of the selfobject analyst through the process of transmuting internalization. (Kohut postulated that transmuting internalization may take place without the patient undergoing at least apparent frustration. See Chapter 5.) The accruing of self structure through this process facilitates the development of the selfobject transferences. The reader may question my communicating to Mr. V. my recognition of his assertiveness, and thereby, furthering his grandiosity, as Mr. V.'s grandiosity was already quite blatant. In answer to this I would like to suggest that Mr. V.'s grandiosity, which emerged as a global defensive reaction to the threat of the loss of self cohesiveness, was qualitatively different from his more focused and directed suspicion of my intentions. Mr. V. had indicated that he was open to finding out about me. He was at least allowing the possibility of reconsidering his grandiose conviction that everyone was out to take from him.

I said, "I think I see what you're saying–that I would like to get as much money as possible. That getting money is more important than anything else."

Mr. V. said, "Why not? I look at everybody that way. Why should you be different? Nobody wants to know my problems." He sat down easily in the chair and cupped both hands around his face and began rubbing his eyes in what seemed like an attempt to keep from falling asleep. "It's my philosophy. People are out for themselves. The system is corrupt. . . ." Mr. V. continued to rub his eyes. His voice softened as he tried to stifle a yawn. "I'm scared. I'm only 32 and I feel my life is over. I don't know what to do." Mr. V. closed his eyes. "I'm getting sleepy. . . ." With a sudden burst of alertness, Mr. V. then sat forward in the chair. "You would have a different feeling if I sued you. If you didn't help me after I paid you. Yeah, if I got my money back and maybe more. You would do everything to protect yourself from me!"

I understood Mr. V.'s explosive burst as the defensive mobilization of a primitive and invulnerable grandiose self. I was aware that just before his outburst, Mr. V.'s defensiveness had diminished and he had begun to share his feelings of being scared and confused. In those moments I had sensed his longing for relief and understanding. There had been a sleepy, relaxed, and drifting quality in his experience which led me tentatively to postulate the emergence of some form of idealizing merger experience, as evidenced by what had seemed to be a dreamlike longing for relief.

At this point, I wished to communicate my understanding because Mr. V. had revealed a range of experiences through his thoughts, feelings, and ideas. As already emphasized, communication of understanding requires not only an experience-near grasping of what the patient is going through; it also requires some sense of the availability of that experience (the experience in ascendancy) to the patient's own consciousness. Putting it all together, Mr. V. seemed to be communicating: Why should I let myself hope for comfort or help? I've always been deprived and hurt. Nobody ever put me first so why should I think you (the analyst) are any different? If it came to suing for my money, you would think of yourself first.

The task here was to find a way to communicate my understanding thus far of those various themes of Mr. V.'s unfolding experience, in a manner which would not fall short of or go beyond that with which he is in touch.

I said, "I hear that you're thinking that nobody would ever put you first – nobody – including me."

Mr. V. said, "You're damn right." At that moment he closed his eyes, relaxed, leaned back in the chair, and began to speak softly "I've got a headache." Then he added, after a long pause, "I'm too tired – very tired."

Once more Mr. V. seemed to drift into some peaceful dreamlike state. I was struck again by the contrast between my initial extrospective view of Mr. V. as physically strong, coordinated, and powerful, and my experience-near impression of him as physically vulnerable. In fact, as I maintained my immersion into his drifting and sleepy state, I became more aware of an uncoordinated quality in his movements. For example, as he closed his eyes and leaned back in the chair, he nearly knocked the small side table over once again. This time I understood his tipping the table as unintentional and resulting from his inattention to his surroundings. This experience-near understanding was in contrast to my initial fleeting consideration that he had intentionally overturned the table in the first moments of our session. As Mr. V. reached for the falling table, I was aware of his difficulty in reacting quickly and accurately. The table, which tipped slowly, almost hit the floor before he was finally able to catch it after several attempts. Needless to say, my experience-near impression was different from my experience-distant one of Mr. V. as agile and athletic.

In a sleepy voice, with his eyes still closed, Mr. V. said, "I think I should come to therapy for awhile. I guess you will see me."

I said, "Yes, I would like to work with you." (Mr. V. opened his eyes and quickly closed them. He was becoming anxious. He inhaled deeply and began to twist and turn his face from side to side, much as he had done earlier.)

He said, "I can't believe I'm saying what I'm saying. What's your fee?"

I told him what my fee was and added that I had this particular time open for his appointment if it was good for him. Mr. V. said nothing. He began to move restlessly with his eyes closed.

Through my attunement to his experience I got the impression that he was straining to contain his mounting feelings.

Suddenly he stood up, pointed his finger at me and shouted: "Oh! So you are interested in when you can see me. Say it! You want me to come at least twice. Huh? So what other times are O.K.? How many times a week are O.K.? How about twice a day—fourteen times a week?"

I was aware that my adding the information about a suitable time was an intervention which did not evolve from Mr. V.'s experience, nor was it made with the consideration of those aspects of Mr. V.'s experience of which he was aware (in ascendancy). It was, therefore, a disrupting intrusion into the fragile beginning of the establishment of an empathic bond.

The reader might question here how my comment about

the appointment time – even though unrelated to Mr. V.'s experience – could be so disturbing to him. After all, my adding the information about the time seemed to follow logically his question about my fee. Also it is necessary that the patient be informed as to the facts of the analyst's policies, such as the time of fee payments, responsibility regarding payment of missed sessions, length of sessions, vacation scheduling, and so on. A further question could be asked: Am I not exaggerating the impact that the addition of this bit of information made on Mr. V.? Perhaps Mr. V. would have become enraged anyway?

In response to these questions, I would like to suggest the following: **As with explaining and with asking direct questions, the providing of factual information – which does not evolve from an understanding of the patient's experience and does not take into consideration the aspects of his or her experience in ascendancy – will likely cause a disruption either in the formation of an empathic connection or in the empathic selfobject bond that has already been formed.** The severity of the experience of disruption depends on the degree of dissolution or fragmentation of the patient's self. Patients with greater self cohesiveness and more reliable self structure may weather these breaks easily and show a facility to reestablish the empathic tie. Patients like Mr. V., who have severe nuclear defects in the self, are seriously threatened with the loss of cohesiveness at these times and usually have great difficulty in reconnecting with the analyst.

One might ask a further question regarding the content of Mr. V.'s response. How could Mr. V. have come to his idea that I was trying to get him to come more often than the specific hour I offered? I had made no mention of any additional time, and, in fact, I had implied by my statement that I was not sure if the one hour I suggested would be a convenient time for him. Doesn't Mr. V.'s obvious distortion of my communication to him indicate that he might be suffering from more serious pathology than what has been defined as borderline? If this is true, am I not overemphasizing the disruption of the beginning formation of the self-selfobject bond as the major cause of Mr. V.'s explosive behavior? That is, perhaps Mr. V.'s outbursts had occurred as a result of pathological thinking processes?

Certainly at this time I could not know the extent of Mr. V.'s pathology. However, even if it turned out that Mr. V. was very seriously disturbed, and that he characteristically behaved as he had with me, I would maintain that my unempathic intervention was a major factor in his outburst. As discussed earlier, Kohut (1984, pp. 8–9) stressed the importance of maintaining a reliable empathic bond with those patients whose nuclear self has not been sufficiently established (the borderline and psychotic personality organizations). If the empathic connection is maintained, these patients may then use the analyst as a selfobject to build up new defensive structures and to solidify existing ones. As pointed out, disruptions in the developing selfobject transference can be especially debilitating to the structurally deficient patient.

Following Kohut, I understood that Mr. V.'s expectation that I wished to take from him was primarily an attempt to preserve an enfeebled self by preparing for further jeopardy. For example, Mr. V., whatever the circumstances, had experienced being unfairly treated and financially disadvantaged. His recent divorce coupled with his experience of rejection by his cousin, who gave him a deadline to get work and move out, were especially upsetting to him. Mr. V.'s thinking of me as someone who not only would wish to see him at least twice per week but who could potentially ask him to come daily, prepared him for any current or future attempt I might make to get his money. Whereas Mr. V. himself had brought in his expectation of being hurt and disadvantaged, my unempathic intervention had added to his pain, and, therefore, his conviction.

Patients who have extensive nuclear or primary defects in the self, and who subsequently have developed self structure which are, for the most part, defensive rather than compensatory, will, as did Mr. V., tend to anticipate the ways they can be hurt. These defensive reactions may be precipitated by a disruption in the selfobject transference and/or by some negative life circumstance. Once the self-selfobject bond is reestablished and/ or the effects of the traumatic life situation have been at least partially worked through, the patient's need for expecting the worst usually subsides. This can be true even in those cases in which expectations of some injury to the self have become elaborated and fixed as part of what has commonly been referred to in the literature as a delusional system of thinking.

AN EXAMPLE OF DELUSIONAL THINKING: A SELF PSYCHOLOGICAL UNDERSTANDING

[For example] Dr. L., unlike Mr. V., wanted very much to begin treatment with me. He was concerned about his inability to complete a research project which was required of him as research physicist in a large engineering corporation. Dr. L., 39 years of age, had been convinced for over a year that he was going to be poisoned by breathing the air in several of the buildings where he was doing his research. To summarize, Dr. L. had suddenly developed an elaborate system of thinking that led him to believe that certain combinations of air pollutants, if combined with specific chemicals to which he was exposed, would eventually poison him and "deteriorate" his body. Dr. L.'s delusional thinking was organized around a specific aspect of his work. It interfered with his completing his research as he avoided experiments that had to be completed in certain buildings.

Dr. L., a highly intelligent man, had suffered traumatic deprivation throughout his early childhood. He and his older sister had been abandoned by their mother and father when he was 4. He was separated from his sister and placed in a foster home. By 6 years of age he was placed again; at 8 he went to live with his paternal uncle. There were severe primary deficiencies in the development of self structure as seen in his attempts at maintaining cohesiveness through long periods of nightly rocking, masturbation, and hyperactive behavior. He had turned to drugs during adolescence but was able to achieve in his schoolwork and received a college tuition scholarship in his final year of high school. He was gifted in mathematics and was determined to get his doctorate, graduating with honors after ten years of part-time postgraduate study. He was offered and accepted employment from an engineering firm, where he had worked for two years before the acute onset of the delusion.

Unlike his academic achievement, which eventually culminated in the completion of his doctorate, finishing his research had a specific and threatening meaning to him. By virtue of finishing and publishing his research he would be given new responsibilities and promoted from his research position. Promotion would also require him to agree to a time commitment. Also, against his own wishes, Dr. L. had agreed with his wife to have a child upon the completion of his research and when his promotion was finalized.

As treatment proceeded he was able to reconstruct what these commitments meant to him. He was able to associate to many of the relentless and tragic moments of rejection, loneliness, and paralyzing loss which had permeated his childhood and had inevitably occurred at times of emotional closeness. The threat of promotion from his research position and the thought of becoming a father triggered destabilizing, traumatic experiences of inevitable rejection and aloneness. They threatened him with the loss of stabilizing–compensatory structure that had been developed as Dr. L. formed an idealizing bond with his uncle, who had introduced him to the importance of academic achievement and supplied needed mirroring of his considerable abilities to learn.

The transmuting internalization of the functions of this admired significant figure sustained Dr. L. as he devoted himself to academic excellence. Completing his research, and the resulting promotion to a non-research position and becoming a father, severely threatened him with the loss of all that sustained him.*

Dr. L.'s elaborate delusional thinking, which entailed fears of bodily deterioration, can be understood as an attempt to explain (through a misuse of facts, reason, and logic) the relentless paralyzing and destabilizing experiences of bodily disintegration that he had experienced as a child and now feared as an adult. He associated his fears of "deterioration" and being poisoned to memories of numerous childhood experiences of "losing his breath and body sensations," when he and his sister had been left alone and unattended after their alcoholic parents quarreled violently and then left the home for long periods. He remembered the many times his mother and father had threatened to "starve" him and his sister as punishment when they complained about eating. Dr. L. remembered that it was around his feeling of being forced to eat that he first had thoughts of being poisoned. Thoughts of dying had persisted until he was placed with his uncle.

The relevant point here is that Dr. L.'s delusional thinking subsided and finally disappeared as the ongoing structure-building process took place. He was able to uncover his tormenting experiences of childhood within the context of a firmly developed idealizing selfobject transference. Dr. L. was able to

---

*Note the difference between Dr. L.'s idealization of academic success, and Mr. N.'s (Chapter 4) "professional student" attitude toward his studies which preserved a sustaining twinship bond. Learning, for both Dr. L. and Mr. N., maintained sustaining self-selfobject bonds but within different sectors of the self.

build on the sustaining compensatory structure in this pole of the self, and to widen his idealized goals to encompass learning in other than research areas. He was able to finish his research, accept his promotion, and make valuable contributions as an administrator including an innovative plan for the reorganization of the corporation. Similarly, he was able to plan for a child and become very interested in learning about child development.

CONTINUING WITH MR. V.

Having understood the importance of the empathic process in working with severely disturbed patients such as Dr. L., how was it then that I added the point about the possible meeting time when I was very much aware not only of Mr. V.'s fearful expectation of being "ripped off" by having to pay a fee, but also of being asked to come more than once a week to treatment. I was also aware that his first inquiry about my fee had been extremely anxiety-provoking for him and that he had reacted with a surge of defensive grandiosity. Why then, with those experiences in mind, did I not stay with Mr. V.'s experience when he asked me again about the fee, and simply answered him without imposing the further threatening subject of the meeting time?

In considering these questions, I can say that I added the fact about the time as an unconscious (countertransference) attempt to slip this potentially volatile issue past him as quickly as possible. In this way I was unconsciously hoping to bypass what I knew was potentially upsetting to him. My awareness of my countertransference was an opportunity for me again to utilize self-analysis to determine what residues of past influencing experiences were being triggered, causing me to avoid Mr. V.'s volatility.

My task was now to reimmerse myself in Mr. V.'s experience, which still seemed to me to be a kind of conviction that I was out to take advantage of him. I thought it critically important to expand my attunement as much as possible to encompass all the nuances of his experiences, in order to get as accurate an understanding as possible. I thought that in view of Mr. V.'s conviction-like impression of me, any further misunderstanding of his experience may be more than he could tolerate.

I said, "I think you're feeling that I can't wait to talk about the number of sessions—maybe not just talk but talk you into coming more and more and more."

Mr. V. said, "You're damn right." At that moment he relaxed in his chair, closed his eyes again, and stretched his legs forward. "I've got a headache, guess I'm hungry." For some moments he said nothing. Then he slowly stood up and looked at his watch. "I don't want to speak anymore but I'll come back next week, O.K.?"

I said, "Yes, I would like to see you." Mr. V., seemingly unaffected by my response, walked to the door and, without waiting for me, left the office.

Mr. V.'s expectation of my exploiting him had diminished dramatically after I communicated my understanding ("you're feeling that I can't wait to talk . . . you into coming more and more and more"). His reaction indicated for me that I had been able to feel and think my way into his experience with some accuracy. It was only through the patient's response to the communication that the analyst can know whether or not his or her intervention has a degree of accuracy in explaining the patient's behavior. Mr. V. responded positively and seemed to feel understood, as evidenced by his wish to come again the following week. Although he ended the session by seemingly withdrawing into his own world, and walking out without recognition of me, the intensity of his experience was greatly reduced from that which I had sensed during the initial moments of meeting him and at other times during the session.

SUMMARY OF THE INITIAL SESSION

In this discussion of Mr. V.'s initial session, I have attempted to highlight the major transitional points of the session for the purpose of helping the reader follow my moment-to-moment attempts to understand Mr. V. and communicate my understanding to him.

From the first moments Mr. V. was expecting the worst from me. This implied that even before meeting me he had brought into the session his negative expectations. My inability to understand, or to communicate my understanding from an experience-near vantage point during those initial moments led to an intensification of his negative expectations and defensive grandiosity. As I struggled to immerse myself in his experience and was more successful in empathically communicating what I understood his experience to be, he was able to accept my communication and move from his isolated world of grandiosity. In those moments Mr. V. appeared to become less anxious and at times became sleepy and relaxed. His movement into those more peaceful feeling states can be tentatively understood as his being able to derive some soothing comfort from my understanding, and possibly some form of merger bond. This fragile tie, however, was easily disrupted by his expectations that I was interested only in taking his money, as seen when he first inquired about my fee and reacted explosively before I could answer.

By turning to self-analysis (the self-analytic function that I had acquired in my personal analysis), I was able to acknowledge my interfering response and connect it to past experiences, and thereby lessen the intensity of my responses to his reactive grandiose outburst. This process made it possible for me to maintain an immersion into his rapidly shifting affect states, and to come to a beginning experience-near understanding of his delusionlike expectation of "being ripped off."

My communication of my understanding had meaning to Mr. V. and served to help establish an empathic connection, so that by the end of the session he was open to continuing the following week.

His explosive reactive grandiosity indicated a high degree of vulnerability and the need to defend against the loss of self cohesiveness. This suggests primary or nuclear defects in the development of the self. His sleepiness and apparent withdrawal into what seemed to be a private world, disconnected from his surroundings, suggested some form of primitive merger experience.

The developmental level of the selfobject ties provides a tentative understanding of the extent of the patient's pathology. For example, the more archaic or primitive expressions of the self may encompass a variety of magical notions of power and strength which is thought to be derived through depersonalized rituals, incantation, and the like (which are not uncommon to many religious services). Patients who rely heavily on idealized, depersonalized omnipotent objects can be viewed as regressed or developmentally fixed on archaic idealizations. Patients who, like Mr. V., react with cold and paranoid grandiosity can also be understood to have undergone regression or have become developmentally fixed on archaic forms of the grandiose self.

As the empathic connection was re-established the near-delusional quality of Mr. V.'s convictions subsided. This is not unusual even when the patient's thinking process is clearly delusional, as was pointed out with Dr. L. Emphasis was on the experience-near understanding of both Mr. V.'s and Dr. L.'s experience of jeopardy, as expressed by their convictions. It can be noted here that this mode of listening and understanding is in contrast with experience-distant understanding, where the focus might be on questioning, or in some way confronting, the reality of the patient's thinking process.

In the discussion of this session, I have attempted to clarify the experience-near mode of data gathering. It follows that diagnostic questions to determine ego strengths or the extent of pathology can serve to disrupt the emergence of the selfobject transference, and iatrogenically exacerbate, if not create, the pathological condition. **Discussions as to time of sessions, fees, policies regarding vacations, payments of missed sessions, and so on, while important, should be secondary to the concerns of understanding the patient and establishing the empathic selfobject bond. If a firm empathic bond has been established, such discussions can evolve naturally or be introduced with a minimum of disruption.**

CHAPTER 17

Development of the Therapeutic Process: The Case of Mr. V.

The following session with Mr. V. was in the tenth month of treatment. At the time of the session, I had been seeing him once per week. He had obtained work as an electronics salesman and was attending college as a part-time student to complete his bachelor's degree. He was now living by himself in his own apartment.

As with other sessions, the moment-to-moment significant sequences are highlighted as accurately as possible, while confidentiality is protected.

As Mr. V. entered the office, I sensed that he was pleased if not happy. He looked directly at me, smiled, and stretched out his

arm to hand me a check. "Well, here's the check – on time this time –
and I got the amount right – right?"

I got the impression that Mr. V. was proudly letting me in
on his successful effort to pay the correct fee and pay it on time.
Through expanding my attunement to his experience, I also
sensed that Mr. V. was not only exhibiting his pleasurable
experience of accomplishment, but wished me to take notice that
he was feeling proud about being able to share his feelings of
accomplishment. In other words, Mr. V. was also feeling proud
about feeling proud. This point may seem somewhat convoluted
and unnecessary. However, I would again wish to repeat the
suggestion that a full understanding of the patient's experience
can come about only if we are finely attuned to as many of the
shades or nuances as possible.

I wished, therefore, to recognize his achievement at paying
the accurate amount and doing so on time, as well as his experience of satisfaction and enjoyment in the exhibiting of his
success. I felt that both of these aspects of his experience were
available to his consciousness – that is, were in ascendancy.

I said, "I certainly see you have it right – also, I see it's a happy feeling
for you." Mr. V. smiled broadly and quickly pointed in succession to
his sports jacket and pants. "How do you like these? – tailor-made –
first time I ever had anything tailor-made." Still smiling, he began to
rub the material of his jacket lapel. "See this – one hundred percent
imported wool!"

From his experience I got the impression that Mr. V. was
accepting my intervention and that he felt a heightened freedom
to exhibit his spontaneity, enthusiasm, and satisfaction. He was
risking more and more the exposure of his exhibitionistic/gran-
diose self, as he grew increasingly able to experience me as an
understanding and mirroring selfobject. I understood this change

as evidence of a developing mirror selfobject transference in the narrower sense of the term, which is ". . . the therapeutic reinstatement of that normal phase of the development of the grandiose self in which the gleam in the mother's eye, which mirrors the child's exhibitionistic display, and other forms of maternal participation in and response to the child's narcissistic-exhibitionistic enjoyment confirm the child's self-esteem and, by a gradually increasing selectivity of these responses, begin to channel it into realistic directions" (Kohut 1971, p. 116).

I said, "I see what you mean – one hundred percent – no blends – and tailor-made – kinda like a first." Mr. V. happily turned to show me the back of his jacket. "See here how the jacket falls. I like it."

I nodded my head to indicate that I did see. After some moments of modeling his jacket, he slowly sat in the chair.

It can be pointed out that I attempted to maintain my immersion into Mr. V.'s experience even though at one point he asked me to tell him my personal (experience-distant) opinion of his tailor-made pants and jacket. Again, my emphasis was on understanding from the experience-near vantage point. Mr. V.'s wish to know my opinion was only a part of his total experience of exhibiting his satisfaction about this choice of clothing, and about its design. My response, therefore, was intended to encompass many aspects of his experience that I thought were available to his consciousness (in ascendancy). If I had responded only to his wish for my opinion, I would have bypassed aspects of his enthusiasm. However, it may be asked, did I relate at all to his request for my opinion? Where was it in my response ("I see what you mean – one hundred percent – no blends – and tailor-made – kinda like a first")? Again, I can answer that I did relate to this question within the context of my understanding of the nuances of Mr. V.'s experience. Mr. V.'s question, "How do you like these?" (referring to his pants and jacket) was an expression of his enthusiasm within his shifting overall experience, which moved quickly to his enthusiasm about the quality of the tailoring and the material.

The first part of my response ("I see what you mean . . .") reflected my understanding of the overall satisfaction that was expressed in his question. The latter part of my communication (" . . . one hundred percent – no blends – and tailor-made – kinda like a first") reflected my understanding of the specifics of his enthusiasm, which centered on his experience of the quality and details of the tailoring as well as on his awareness that tailoring was new for him. As stated, Mr. V.'s heightened enthusiasm that followed my intervention indicated that the communication of my understanding was meaningful to him. It can be assumed, therefore, that my understanding of Mr. V.'s experience had at least some degree of accuracy.

My communication of my understanding of the specifics of Mr. V.'s experience was not an attempt to mirror as an effort to gratify Mr. V.'s need for a confirming response (Wolf 1976, 1988). Rather it was a first step in recognizing the extent and quality of his mirroring needs, which would be analyzed later as the mirroring needs further emerged. This issue will be taken up in the final chapter.

We can see that the primary development of the mirror selfobject transference (in the narrower sense) is qualitatively different from Mr. V.'s mobilized reactive grandiose self, which had been evident in the initial session. This development indicated that Mr. V. had over time become more trustful in revealing his accomplishments, and expressing his satisfaction and joy at these accomplishments. Whereas the opening sequence of this session was not the first time he had shared moments of successes with me, it was the first time that he did so with enthusiasm. It can be assumed that Mr. V.'s developing capacity to accept my understanding, and his evolving selfobject requirements for mirroring of his emerging grandiose self, were indications that he was acquiring compensatory structure in this sector of the self (through the process of transmuting internalization).

Mr. V. went on to say, "Everybody at school today was really impressed with my new look. You know, they're not running away from me. Some of the students actually try to understand me – I mean this really blows my mind. It goes against my feeling that everyone is out for themselves. If I answer questions in class, some students really try to understand what I mean. Then I feel that I've lost my identity. I am afraid I'll have nothing left if I like them – I'm so sleepy – When I think this way, it's either sleep or fight."

Mr. V. closed his eyes, leaned back in the chair, and stretched his arms and legs. "God, this is peaceful – drifting – peaceful so peaceful – like becoming part of the universe." After a long pause Mr. V. sat up slowly. "I had that sudden urge to scream again. I really wanted to knock over this table and jump up . . . like another one of those times we talked about, when I feel like I'm coming apart. It's hard to believe this really happens over and over again."

Mr. V. seemed intent on understanding his dramatically shifting experience. This was not the first time he had been curious about his sudden bursts of powerful feelings. However, I got the impression that there was a heightened vitality and spontaneity in his curiosity that day. I understood this as an expression of his evolving exhibitionistic/grandiose self, already seen in the spontaneous assertive display of his choice of clothing and in his proud feeling of paying the correct fee on time. Clearly Mr. V.'s curiosity was in ascendancy, as was his requirement of my mirroring attention and understanding. This emergence of his exhibitionistic needs indicated the initial unfolding of a mirror transference in the narrower sense.

I said, "I hear how important understanding yourself is to you – how much you are thinking about the ways you feel." Mr. V. nodded his head in agreement and said, "That's right. For some reason I am interested in understanding what's happening inside of me, but I'm not clear why it is important–I don't have to come anymore. My cousin can't force me anymore. I have my own apartment. I must be getting my hopes up about life." Mr. V. became anxious. "Maybe I can do a lot of things. My teachers tell me I'm smart. I could be a teacher: I always wanted to be college professor. It's confusing. I feel stupid–don't know who I am."

DEFENSIVE REACTIONS AGAINST THE
DEVELOPMENT OF THE MIRROR TRANSFERENCE

As the primary mirror selfobject transference was unfolding, Mr. V. was becoming more in touch with his heretofore repressed ambitions and goals. Characteristic of the development of the mirror selfobject transference is the remobilization of unmet mirroring needs. The patient will begin to recover the debilitating aspects of traumatic past experiences, which become mobilized and telescoped into present analogous situations. Patients inevitably experience anxiety as this mobilization occurs. The anxiety may be manifested as vague discomfort, shame, embarrassment, and/or confusion. A variety of defense mechanisms such as repression, denial, and disavowal may be employed to prevent any further mobilization of the grandiose self.

[For example] Mr. Q., a 33-year-old man who had suffered severe childhood trauma, sought treatment because he became depressed and went through periods of inactivity each time he achieved significant success in his work as an executive with a nationally known advertising firm. Mr. Q. was seen in psychoanalysis by a colleague in weekly supervision with me. Even though he was appointed to a high-level executive position and was praised publicly by the officers of the corporation, he was unable to experience pleasure or even satisfaction at such times; in addition, he would be worried that he had somehow committed serious errors in his business negotiations, which he was unaware of but would discover at some future time. For the most part he denied any real ability to carry out his job and considered himself a "fraud." After a brief period during which there was an initial firm development of the idealizing selfobject transference, Mr. Q. began to develop a secondary mirror transference (in the narrower sense). He eventually became able to get in touch with and work through his intense anxiety around exposing his considerable talents and abilities.

Mr. Q.'s initial denial of the quality and meaning of his achievements, and his disavowal of those exhibitionistic aspects of the self, were defensive efforts at preventing the development of the mirror transference and with it the revival of associations to past traumatic experiences.

As with Mr. Q., Mr. V.'s anxious feeling of confusion when considering goals and ambitions was understandable in view of his developing mirror selfobject transference and the accompanying anxiety.

I wanted to communicate my understanding of Mr. V.'s experience of anxiety, which I considered to be precipitated by the recovery and unfolding of his ambitions and goals (as well as his awareness of his potential for fulfilling them). This communication can be considered a first step in the explaining process that introduces the patient to the thought that certain disturbing genetic influences, can determine behavior and interfere with development.

As previously discussed, explaining is more experience-distant than the first step of the treatment process, which is understanding. However, explaining can deepen as well as strengthen the selfobject bond, and can lead to a lessening of anxiety as the internalization of the anxiety-relieving functions of the selfobject analyst takes place.

I said to Mr. V., "Just as you were considering your teachers' praise of you, and the many things you could do, you began to feel that something was wrong–that you were stupid–confused."

Mr. V. listened intently, then closed his eyes and leaned back in his chair. After some moments he said, "Yes, it's as I said, I'm getting my hopes up. I'm really scared when I think about it. It's like being a fool or something. I've always felt like this. Somehow I know that. Don't get your hopes up." He began to shift nervously and rub his eyes, which he kept closed. After some moments he looked at me. "That's it. Can't think anymore. I know there's more, but at least I didn't feel like jumping up and knocking over anything. I just feel stuck."

Maintaining my immersion into his experience and attempting to expand my attunement to its nuances, I sensed that Mr. V. felt understood by my intervention and was concentrating even more intensely on understanding the dynamics of his current emotional state. He also began to consider that his current feelings were similar to those of the past ("I've always felt like this"). While he was anxious about continuing his exploration he was proud that he did not feel destructive.

I understood his strength of focus and his pursuit of understanding to be a direct result of his feeling understood by my communication. As suggested, explanations can deepen the selfobject connection and therefore facilitate the development of the selfobject transferences.

It is important that the analyst maintain an immersion into the patient's experience (in ascendancy) throughout the development of the selfobject transference, and communicate an understanding of this experience as the development occurs. This provides the patient with a continuous experience of being understood, which facilitates the further development of the selfobject transference.

I said, "You're telling me more and more just how much you're putting things together even though it is not easy." Mr. V. quickly replied,

"Not easy? That's an understatement. You're right, I am pushing my mind to understand things, but don't think you really know how difficult this is."

Mr. V. seemed angry at first and then saddened by my intervention. Although it seemed that he did accept my understanding that he was making greater efforts to think through his difficulties, he did not feel I understood the depth of his difficulty.

Mr. V. was accurate as to my not really understanding the degree of difficulty his struggle had for him. It is important to recognize that my error here was my lack of attunement to the level of his difficulty in thinking through the problem, and not that I was unaware that he was having difficulty. After considering possible countertransference interferences, I thought my difficulty was primarily a technical one. Picking up and keeping in mind the patient's experience is no easy task especially when the patient undergoes a sudden shifting from one affect state to another. For example, Mr. V. had moved from experiencing anxiety to feeling proud that he did not become destructive. I was focusing more on his feeling proud at the expense of being attuned to his struggle.

Out of curiosity I was tempted to review the session to myself to locate where I had technically failed to focus on the depth of his struggle. However, to have done so would have tended to remove me from the moment that Mr. V. was sharing, which might have created a further breach in the empathic bond. I am suggesting here that even brief excursions into the analyst's own thoughts, which are removed from the patient's experience, can serve to disrupt the empathic connection. This also holds true when the analyst is exploring countertransference interferences (self analysis). However, unlike my curiosity about technique, the self-analytic function is often necessary to reestablish empathy.

Thinking and feeling my way into Mr. V.'s experience, I picked up not only his initial anger and then his sadness, but also his effort to explain to me how I failed to tune in on his painful difficulty. His communication of his disappointment in me was a dramatic contrast to his earlier defensive grandiose reactions. I understood this difference as evidence of the transmuting internalization of compensatory structure which provided Mr. V. with a greater degree of self-cohesiveness and a degree of invulnerability to breaks in the selfobject connection. Mr. V.'s disappointment indicated that he was experiencing a loss of me as a mirroring selfobject at a crucial point, when he was beginning to consider painful connections.

I wanted to communicate my understanding in order to repair the disruption, and to thereby facilitate the further development of the selfobject transference. It can be reemphasized that there is no such condition as perfect empathy. Although we attempt as much as possible to expand our attunement to the patient's experience, there will always be times when the patient's fluctuating affective states will be difficult and/or impossible to detect; this may be the case no matter how well the analyst maintains an immersion in the patient's experience. The repairing of these inevitable empathic breaches, by analyzing them, is a valuable and essential part of the treatment process. For example, if the analyst can remain attuned to and communicate an understanding of the patient's experience of disruption, the patient can begin to associate to and work through those aspects of past traumatic unempathic experiences that have been telescoped in the selfobject transference. Throughout this process, structure-building occurs through the transmuting internalization of the empathic functions of the selfobject analyst.

I said to Mr. V., "I missed what you're going through deep down. It's much more than not being 'easy'." Mr. V. said nothing. After a long pause he again closed his eyes and leaned back in his chair. He said softly, "I'm getting very sleepy again. I didn't want you to say that. You really want to understand me. You don't mind admitting when you're off the mark."

I felt at this moment that Mr. V. was experiencing a mixture of anxiety with feelings of satisfaction, appreciation, comfort, and some admiration of me as a result of my understanding. I postulated that he was also experiencing some tentative idealization of me as an understanding and soothing selfobject. Should this be true, perhaps he would be able in time to develop a stable idealizing selfobject transference and acquire reliable compensatory structure in the idealizing sector of the self.

At this point it could be surmised that Mr. V.'s diminished defensiveness and greater tolerance for my empathic failure indicated that compensatory structure had been formed in the sector of his exhibitionistic self.

The importance of the development of reliable compensatory structure in the various poles of the self has repeatedly been emphasized by Kohut. The accruing of compensatory self structure through the bit-by-bit transmuting internalization of the empathic functions of the selfobject analyst brings about a functional rehabilitation of the self by strengthening one or more poles or sectors. This strengthening process is integral to the total analytic process and allows for further development of the selfobject bonds in the treatment. Concomitantly, this development is reflected outside of treatment as the patient widens his or her selection of selfobjects to meet changing mirroring and idealizing needs, with the evolving of new goals and ideals.

REACTIONS TO THE IDEALIZING TRANSFERENCE

Having gained an awareness of what Mr. V. was experiencing, and a very tentative understanding that there was some evidence of an expression of idealizing needs, I wanted as much as possible to allow for whatever development might take place. Kohut (1971) has specifically taught that when an idealizing transference begins to develop, ". . . there is only one correct analytic attitude: to accept the admiration" (p. 264). Kohut also warns that an analyst who has not come to terms with his or her own grandiose self may in some way reject the patient's idealization, as part of a defensive effort to prevent the stimulation of repressed grandiose fantasies. If the analyst's defensive attitude is chronic, there will be an interference in the establishment of a workable idealizing transference. Then the transmuting internalization in that area of the patient's self, which takes place through the step-by-step working-through processes, will be prevented.

There are common responses which may indicate the analyst's resistance to allowing the patient's idealizing selfobject transference to unfold. These are: (1) the assumption that there is always hostility behind the patient's wish to admire the analyst and (2) the assumption that in order to maintain a friendly rapport with the patient, the analyst must respond to the admiration with some correction of the patient's reality.

Regarding the first of these assumptions, that there is always underlying hostility behind the admiration, the analyst would necessarily focus on the admiration as defensive. Interventions, therefore, would be made to uncover the hidden hostility with all of its associative meanings. Such interventions would communicate to the patient that the admiration was a defensive "cover-up" and not important in itself as a continuation of previously thwarted development. The emerging idealizing needs of the patient, as reflected in the unfolding of the idealizing selfobject transference, would not be understood. The patient, therefore, would not experience being understood and would tend to limit further expression of these particular self needs.

The second of these common responses, correcting the

reality of the patient's admiration in order to maintain a friendly rapport, is directed toward reducing the emotional distance which comes about through the patient's elevation of the analyst within the idealizing selfobject transference. The analyst may, for example, remind the patient of his or her own positive attributes at the time the patient is praising the qualities of the analyst. The analyst may also disclaim or in some way modify the patient's adulation. For example, the analyst might lightly joke about the patient's overestimation of him or her in an attempt to gently correct the patient's reality; or, more directly, the analyst might refute the patient's evaluation as totally or partially incorrect. No matter how subtle or overt the response may be, the patient's needs for idealizing will be prevented from unfolding.

The above broadly defined responses by the analyst to the idealizing needs of the patient may be firmly anchored in theory. Therefore, the countertransference components of the response may be further disguised insofar as the analyst can theoretically justify the interventions. However, it also follows that analysts who may have resolved interferences in their self development may hold theoretical views that call for interventions that interfere with the development of the idealizing selfobject transference. For example, the assumption that idealization is a defense against underlying hostile impulses is a commonly held experience-distant conceptualization which has its roots in drive/conflict theory.

The assumption that the analyst must correct the reality of the patient's idealization in order to maintain a friendly rapport is founded on ego-based psychological concepts, which focus the treatment on temporary reality testing and on establishing a working alliance in which the patient's ego is engaged in a mutual problem-solving relationship with the analyst.

Returning to Mr. V.'s admiration of me as someone who

really wanted to understand him, the question can be asked: How does one accept the idealizing experience of the patient, as Kohut suggested? If we keep in mind the rule of thumb of understanding the patient through the vantage point of an empathic immersion into his or her experience, we can easily answer the question.

Mr. V.'s experience seemed to be one in which he was feeling admiration for me while at the same time desiring to share that feeling with me as a verbal statement requiring no response.

Unlike the patient's mirroring needs, which require the selfobject analyst to acknowledge and communicate an understanding of the patient's experience of success and accomplishments, the patient's idealizing needs require only that the selfobject analyst not interfere with the unfolding of the idealizing process. Idealization leads to the selfobject analyst being experienced as the consistent, powerful, and protective parental image of which the patient was developmentally deprived.

Kohut's recommendation that the analyst accept the idealization is based not only on the patient's need for the continuation of a developmental process, but also on the fact that the idealizing process can only take place in its own time and without attempts by the analyst to promote or discourage it. **Therefore, I wanted to communicate my acceptance of Mr. V.'s admiration by respectfully listening and remaining silent.**

Mr. V. continued, "I don't remember anybody really giving a damn when I was growing up – maybe you're the only one – I don't think I can open my eyes – so sleepy. I see these beautiful colors – I know about yoga meditation. If I close my eyes, I can sometimes keep that beautiful blue color for a little while. My mother is in here somewhere – maybe I trusted her. I don't mean my real mother. I think I was adopted at birth but they [adopted parents] died when I was around 3. Then foster homes – don't know how many." Mr. V. began to shift his body anxiously. He opened his eyes and began to breathe heavily as he spoke. "I guess that's what happens. When I give up my blue light, every time, I feel I can't take a deep breath."

Mr. V. was again intently thinking about his experiences in the moment and how they were related to those of the past. I began to get some tentative understanding of what Mr. V.'s closing his eyes meant to him. He seemed to be attempting to provide himself with some comfort through a form of limited meditation. I also tentatively understood his revelation of those aspects of his thinking about meditation, as resulting from his beginning to experience me as a comforting idealized selfobject.

I also thought it significant that even though Mr. V. experienced considerable anxiety, as evidenced by his symptomatic breathing, he did not return to his meditation, nor did he indicate that he had the impulse to react explosively in his characteristic grandiose manner. This further indicated that Mr. V. had in these moments been able to experience some comfort and relief through the understanding I provided.

Thus far in this session, Mr. V. had experienced severe anxiety as he revealed aspects of traumatic experiences in both the exhibitionistic and idealizing poles of the self. His anxiety about getting his hopes up was specific to the unfolding of his grandiose self. His anxiety over thinking about the loss of his mother, and the repeated losses of his adoptive and foster parents, can be understood to be specific to the tragic disillusionments he had inevitably suffered during the early phases of idealization.

It can be surmised by the intensity of his anxiety, his reactive behavior, and attempts at comforting himself through meditation, that there had been damage to those sectors of the self. Nevertheless, Mr. V. at this point in the treatment was making considerable effort to understand the meaning of his reactions to current life circumstances, and how those reactions related to and reflected past traumatic experiences.

The moment-to-moment accruing of understanding that I achieved through expanding my attunement to his experiences (which were continually affected by the mutually influencing intersubjective process) allowed me to "bring forward" my ongoing understanding of Mr. V. as the session continued. For example, as Mr. V. was sharing his thoughts about his meditative attempts to comfort himself, my accrued understanding — which now included the meaning that Mr. V.'s experience in discussing his difficulties had for him, and also included awareness of his anxiety levels and of the pervasiveness of his childhood traumas — made it possible for me to understand even more fully the difficulty he was experiencing. Just as I focused on expanding my attunement to what Mr. V. was experiencing, at the same time I came to an expanded understanding of the dynamics of his behavior and a greater clarity as to the genetic (historical) factors involved. With a more complete understanding I would, therefore, be able to make more meaningful communications (interpretations), and thereby deepen the selfobject tie and promote the further development of the selfobject transference. However, it can be emphasized that no matter what the breadth and depth of the analyst's ongoing understanding of the patient's suffering, the analyst should not assume he or she knows what the patient is experiencing. For example, with patients like Mr. V., the analyst — having gained an understanding of the scope of the childhood deprivation — may assume that the patient's recounting of past traumas is more disturbing to the patient than it actually is. The tendency to overestimate the patient's experience is as much an error in attunement as to underestimate it, as occurred earlier with Mr. V.

Now that I was more informed, I wanted to communicate my understanding. Even though I had a wider knowledge of Mr. V.'s mental life, I did not want to communicate more than that which I empathically sensed Mr. V. could understand, from those experiences and awarenesses in his consciousness or those which were likely to be available to his consciousness. As earlier described, ascendant experiences may be a mix of experiences and awarenesses that are carried forward from moment to moment. **Interventions and/or interpretations which are directed to that which seems clearest in ascendancy are more likely to be understood by the patient, and therefore more likely to further the treatment process and to facilitate the revealing unconscious material.**

I am calling this to the reader's attention as self psychology has been accused of avoiding dealing with the patient's unconscious because of the focus on the experience-near understanding and explaining treatment process.

Remaining immersed in Mr. V.'s experience, I thought that his anxiously sharing his awareness of the importance to him of his comforting attempts at meditation was his experience in ascendancy. He was clearly entrusting me with how he was able to derive comfort in his life. Within the context of his developing idealization of me, he had begun for the first time to consider the tragic events of his life. This was tentatively understood by me as a further risking and exposing of his vulnerability. I wanted to communicate my understanding of the pain he had suffered, and, in a limited way, to interpret (explain) that his meditation or "blue light" experience had historical significance.

I said, "More and more you're letting me in on the pain you have endured. I understand now how the "blue light" has been so important in your life. Mr. V. nodded his head in agreement. I was aware that he immediately began to breathe more easily; and then, after several moments of silence, he began again to shift uneasily and breathe irregularly. He said, "I had the feeling of wanting to tell you more, and then I thought I couldn't. But I guess I can." At this point Mr. V. described in detail an instance of sexual abuse around the age of seven during one of his foster home placements. He remembered that he was playing with a relative of a friend of his foster mother. This man tied his hands and legs as part of an apparent game, and then undressed him. At this time Mr. V. remembered only the confusion, numbness, and pain of being penetrated. He was fairly certain that it had occurred more than once. Somehow the foster agency had found out about the abuse, and he was placed in another foster home.

Mr. V. wondered if he had always felt "numb" as a child. He never knew his real mother and had only some vague awareness of his adopted parents, whom he was told had died of some illness. He wondered if they really had died. Perhaps they just wanted to get rid of him, he thought, and so they just gave him away. Mr. V. said he thought it really made no difference what had happened. It was all the same—numbness throughout his many foster home placements.

Mr. V. imagined his real mother to have been as beautiful as his "blue light." It was as if he were waiting for her to show up one day and say that she was sorry. He remembered that in his foster home placements he had made cardboard houses and cut-out figures of animals and people. He would then pretend that his mother and the police were searching for him because he was stolen and they were trying to get him back. Mr. V. was curious that he did not remember any fantasy about his father being one of the people who would come to his rescue. He was aware, however, that even before the sexual abuse he had tended to be fearful of men when they attempted to speak and to play games with him.

Mr. V. told me that there were many feelings and thoughts that were confusing to him. He wanted to come twice weekly to treatment as he was concerned that the confusion would be "too much," and that he would again reject the friends he had made at school and work. He did not wish to "throw away" the gains he had made, and was especially concerned that he would become discouraged with school and not follow through on his plans to get his degree. His concern was heightened as he had recently become more successful in his job as a salesman and had been offered a position as a district manager.

Though Mr. V. anticipated difficulty in sharing with me the relentless traumas he had suffered as a child, he was able to do so with far less anxiety than before. I sensed, as he delved into the tragic events of his childhood, that he now welcomed my listening and seemed more capable of revealing painful details. This suggested that he was relying more on me as a comforting selfobject and moving away from his dependency on meditation – that is, on the "blue light."

As the idealizing selfobject transference emerged, I was aware that Mr. V. desired me to listen as he spoke of the tragedies of his life, and, in a sense, to share the burden of them. However, it was difficult for me to stay in Mr. V.'s experience while he revealed the severity of those tragic events. I emphasize the events instead of the patient's experience because it was my reactions to Mr. V.'s descriptions of abuse and loss that, at times, removed me from his experience. I felt both sadness and anger and was aware that I was tempted to make some consoling remark, and to ask questions to satisfy my curiosity and perhaps relieve my own disquieting feelings.

But am I not really implying that my experience-distant attention and reaction to Mr. V.'s description of the traumatic events of his childhood was an error in the treatment, and one which could have been avoided? In other words, were not my reactions – which removed me from Mr. V.'s experience, at least in part – symptomatic of an interfering countertransference? I would answer yes, but with some qualification.

Without getting into the debatable meanings of countertransference (unconscious), evoked (conscious), and provoked reactions, I would like to emphasize that there is no analyst who has been perfectly analyzed. There are always unconscious influences that more or less determine our experience, as well as our reactions to our experience. This is true even though we may be conscious of what we are experiencing.

Being aware of what we are experiencing is important in alerting us to interferences in maintaining empathy. However, it does not necessarily follow that simply being conscious of an experience means that there are no unconscious disturbing influences. This point was illustrated earlier when I described my initial negative reactions to Mr. V., which I was aware of and which were, in part, triggered by residues of unconscious and incompletely worked-through childhood traumas.

This point is especially relevant in discussing my reactions of sadness and anger when Mr. V. described the abuse and deprivations he had suffered as a child. It goes without saying that any analyst with a minimal potential for empathy would be saddened and angered at the abuse Mr. V. had suffered. Even so, I would like to repeat that if the analyst's reactions are such that they tend to remove him or her from what the patient is experiencing, then the analyst is more than likely being influenced by unconscious derivatives. In such a case, the triggering of unresolved unconscious aspects of the analyst's own past traumatic experiences may claim his or her attention and thereby disrupt the empathic immersion into the patient's experience.

This does not imply that the analyst cannot or should not feel strongly about abuse and deprivation. Nor does it imply that, if successfully analyzed, the analyst will arrive at some stereotypically appropriate state of objectivity. It simply means that, no matter how the analyst might feel about such deprivations, he or she will be able to remain in the patient's experience.

Though I was distracted at times from focusing on Mr. V.'s experience, I was able to resist the temptation to relieve my anxiety through asking questions or expressing some personal concern about his suffering. I also think I was at least partially successful in remaining with and acknowledging the various mixtures of his shifting experiences. On the whole I had the impression that he felt understood, in that, as previously pointed out, he seemed to welcome and be relieved by my silent listening.

Mr. V. said, "I'm even more surprised that I haven't jumped up after telling you this. I don't really know if I've ever told anyone this before. Maybe a little bit of it. Guess I can tell you because you came into focus as someone who cares." Mr. V. began to smile. "It really is like you're coming into focus – like I'm seeing you differently somehow."

I understood Mr. V.'s wish to recount the details of his childhood traumas, and to express his changing perception of me, as further evidence of the development of an idealizing selfobject transference. He was experiencing me as someone in whom he could confide. He explained that he felt he could share his past because I was "coming into focus" as someone who cared.

I suggest that Mr. V.'s experience of me as caring was a product of the entire empathic treatment process. The treatment allowed Mr. V. to begin to work through his resistances against establishing an empathic connection. It can be postulated that Mr. V. was beginning to internalize (transmuting internalization) my functions as a listening and understanding selfobject.

As Mr. V.'s idealizing needs emerged, he experienced me as providing the emotional comfort and understanding that made it possible for him to confide in me. It is important to note that pointing out his considerable analytic input would have been an error in that it would have disrupted the developing idealizing selfobject transference. **Kohut has warned that it would be deleterious to point out the assets of the patient when the patient's idealizing selfobject transference is developing** (1971, p. 264). To do so would be an error in understanding the idealizing needs of the patient, and/or evidence of some difficulty on the part of the analyst to accept the patient's idealization.

Whereas at this point in the treatment Mr. V.'s experience in ascendancy seemed to be a developing idealization, I sensed that he was also feeling a moment of proud success in coming to an awareness of his different view of me. However, Mr. V.'s momentary grandiose and exhibitionistic expression seemed to be a kind of mixture within the context of the emerging idealizing selfobject transference.

Again, I am highlighting the importance of the analyst's expanding attunement to the nuances of the patient's shifting and unfolding experience, to make it possible to achieve a more accurate understanding of the complexities of the patient's needs and behavior. It is only through such experience-near data collecting that the analyst can communicate the most meaningful understanding. For example, having picked up an aspect of exhibitionistic expression in ascendancy within the context of the idealizing selfobject transference, I thought it important to include a recognition of this nuance without disturbing the idealizing process. To recognize or mirror the patient's exhibitionistic expression is a communication of the analyst's understanding of the patient's own attempts at understanding. Specifically, I wanted to communicate my recognition of his analytic awareness that I was "coming into focus" as a caring person. At the same time I wished to include an acceptance of his idealization.

I responded to Mr. V.'s statement that he was seeing me "as someone who cares" by saying, "Yes, I see."

This recognition (mirroring) of Mr. V.'s exhibitionistic expression within the context of the idealizing selfobject transference may be contrasted to the recognition at the beginning of the session, when there was little or no evidence of a developing idealizing selfobject transference.

Through expanding attunement to the patient's shifting experiences, the analyst will become aware of the beginning development of secondary selfobject transferences within the predominant primary selfobject transference configuration. Shifts may be gradual, as was Mr. V.'s slowly emerging idealizing transference. As a rule, patients who have suffered less damage to the various sectors of the self are less resistant to developing selfobject transferences. With these patients, shifts to secondary selfobject transferences may be more rapid.

Expanding attunement to the initial shifts in a patient's experience is important if the analyst is to adequately understand the emerging selfobject needs of the patient, and to make appropriate interventions that allow for the continuing development of the selfobject transferences.

Mr. V. seemed to accept my intervention ("Yes, I see"), and enthusiastically went on to say: "It's really curious how the mind works – at least how mine does. I feel like I can tell you more and more and no matter what I would say you would listen. You know how freeing that is. Maybe this sounds crazy, but I just had the thought of a little child running around babbling, freely practicing how to make sounds – feeling safe enough to make any sound – any sound at all. I think I missed having that – I mean, I know I missed it."

I understood Mr. V.'s experience of a greater freedom to share his thoughts and ideas with me as added evidence of the development of the idealizing selfobject transference. I also understood his continuing to think about and understand his changing experience and view of me, as well as his expressed enthusiasm and curiosity, as evidence of the reemergence of the mirror selfobject transference. However, I had the impression that the idealizing selfobject transference was still the overriding self-selfobject configuration. Mr. V. was experiencing an early form of idealization which could be described as a longing for nonjudgmental freedom to say anything and make any sound he wished.

It seemed that both the expanding exhibitionistic and heightened idealizing components were in ascendancy. I therefore wished to communicate my understanding thus far. Again I wanted to include my recognition of Mr. V.'s growing motivation and effort to understand (the exhibitionistic self), without disturbing the developing idealizing selfobject transference.

I said nothing but simply nodded my head in recognition to indicate I understood what he was saying.

Although it may seem unnecessary to pursue why I chose this nonverbal way of communicating, I would like to suggest that my choice of nonverbal mirroring arose out of my awareness that Mr. V. felt understood by my previous verbal intervention and, therefore, that my continuing recognition of his expanding effort to understand the complexities of his thoughts and feelings required very little emphasis. To say it somewhat differently, I experienced Mr. V.'s ongoing experience of me as an understanding idealized selfobject. To verbalize again the fact that I understood would not only be an unnecessary emphasis but would unempathically ignore the extent of Mr. V.'s understanding.

The question might be asked, how does one communicate this nonverbal nuance of understanding if the patient, unlike Mr. V., is lying down and therefore not facing the analyst? I suggest that if the analyst can feel free from theoretical constructs that focus on experience-distant and therefore exclusively verbal interventions, there can be a more flexible communication that captures the essence of what the patient is experiencing; this would include whatever experience is continually being "brought forward" from previous moments. For example, if Mr. V. were using the couch and lying down, I might have communicated my understanding by voicing some commonly recognized sounds or utterances as we all do now and then in social communication to indicate we understand. The important point is that our communications should be tailored to reflect as much as possible the understanding we gain from the collective experiences of the patient.

After my nonverbal intervention, Mr. V. seemed even more motivated to continue his thinking about his newfound experience of freedom. He repeated that he wished to come more often to treatment even though it would be a financial hardship. He did not want to risk losing the gains he had made. He was "feeling better about himself," but was aware that he had suffered many things as a child and that he now had many problems which could undermine his hopes. In fact, Mr. V. had been having frequent thoughts of "picking up and leaving" his job and treatment. Although things were going well at work and at school, he often felt in a rage and had many destructive wishes, such as stealing on his job and cheating at school.

He also said that there were many other "serious" things on his mind which sometimes worried him and at other times did not seem to bother him. However, he did not want to speak about them today.

He then wondered about coming more often and asked me if I also thought it was important. I agreed with him. I said that his coming more often would give us more time to be on top of things and to understand them in greater depth. Mr. V. thought he could afford only two sessions per week. We decided on a time, and then as he stood to leave he shook his head and said, "I can't believe that I'm doing this!"

CHAPTER 18

More Specific Understanding: The Case of Mr. V.

Mr. V. had been able during the first six months of treatment to move away from his initial grandiose reactive behavior, first to the unfolding of a primary mirror selfobject transference in the narrower sense and then to the beginning development of an idealizing selfobject transference. The initial primitive quality of his experience, both in the pole of his grandiose self and that of his idealizing self, suggested that fixations had occurred as a result of severe traumas and damage to both these sectors.

Mr. V.'s capacity to respond positively to treatment was a good prognostic sign that he would be able to continue his development.

TIMES OF DISILLUSIONMENT

To sum up briefly, Mr. V. continued treatment at the rate of two sessions per week for two years, and then increased the frequency to three weekly sessions for five additional years and until treatment was terminated. His total treatment lasted eight years.

The idealizing selfobject transference which unfolded after the primary mirror transference (in the narrower sense) continued to be the predominant selfobject transference configuration for approximately the next year and a half. However, there were times when he became disillusioned, particularly around the issue of paying his monthly fee.

Mr. V. also became disillusioned with me on those occasions when I failed to meet various requests of his, such as changing his appointments, making up time lost when he was late for sessions, immediately returning a telephone call on one occasion, and extending the length of sessions. This latter wish to extend sessions whenever he felt the need intensified after he began having a second weekly session.

In general, Mr. V.'s disillusionment with me as an idealized selfobject occurred when I failed to provide an all-comforting experience for him, and/or when he experienced me as in some way depriving. At these times he suffered severe anxiety (fragmentation), and sometimes reacted explosively as he had at the beginning (reactive mobilization of the grandiose self).

However, I became aware over time that his defensive grandiose outbursts were usually briefer than they had been on previous occasions. I understood this as evidence of Mr. V.'s gradually accruing self structure which made it possible for him to reestablish more quickly the empathic connection. For example, after the first month of twice-weekly sessions, Mr. V. was late in the payment of his fee. There had been considerable analysis of his resentment over paying, and therefore we had some understanding of the meaning of his resentment. When I brought up the subject of payment, Mr. V. immediately became enraged and bitterly snapped, "You'll get the damn money!" However, this rage quickly subsided and he went on to wonder about his response. He did not feel that I was insensitive to his experience, as he thought that my bringing up the subject of the payment was within the context of what he was discussing at the moment. (Mr. V. was considering his financial situation, his debts and so forth at the time.) His sudden realization that he had forgotten the payment surprised him, "made him feel crazy." He therefore reacted explosively. Mr. V. had previously become aware that when threatened, or even when he anticipated becoming threatened, he would strike out as a way of regaining a sense of security and stability in the wake of destabilizing anxiety (fragmentation).

ADDITIONAL HISTORY

Apart from those brief fragmentating periods when there was a breach in the idealizing bond, Mr. V. developed a firm idealizing selfobject transference during the next two years and until the emergence of a stable secondary mirror transference (in the narrower sense).

During this time, Mr. V. elaborated on the many painful aspects of his childhood. He focused on the relentless feelings of emptiness and loneliness which he had suffered throughout the early years of his life. He vividly remembered one of his foster home placements. His foster mother, who was divorced, had two children, a boy of 11 and a girl of 13, who lived with her. Mr. V. had shared a room with her son whom he remembered as trying to comfort him, especially at night when Mr. V. had difficulty sleeping, and/or when he was awakened with night terrors.

The feelings of trust that he experienced with me reminded him of his friend in that foster home who had tried to understand and help him. There were also happy moments with his friend when the focus was not on Mr. V.'s upset and pain. He remembered his learning how to play baseball and basketball during that period of his life. However, everything came to an abrupt end when Mr. V. was sexually abused by his foster mother's boyfriend. He was taken from the home and Mr. V.'s friend went to live with his father in another state. Mr. V. never heard from him again.

Mr. V. could not remember the aftermath of his abuse and the breakup of the foster family. He never felt that this particular foster mother had been very affectionate to him, and he thought she had wanted to care for him only because of the money. Mr. V. guessed that this had been the beginning of a series of foster homes, which all seemed to run together in his memory.

Mr. V. remembered the "special world" that he had imagined. He would daydream about a forest of friendly animals to whom he gave names. He imagined them to be his brothers and sisters and would talk to them in a special language when he was alone. These fantasies stood side by side with what he described as monster fantasies. A variety of monsters would attack the friendly animals in the forest and either devour them or perform sadistic sexual acts upon them. At times he would masturbate while having these fantasies. Mr. V. also had a special language for the monsters, and when alone he would speak aloud the thoughts of the monsters. Sometimes he would be overheard and laughed at by his foster parents, other foster children with whom he lived, and his classmates.

Mr. V. described himself as a withdrawn child throughout his elementary school years. Although he got passing grades, he was a poor student since his concentration was primarily on his magical private world. Looking back, Mr. V. thought that he had been considered a "quiet" student who was "not too bright." No one had seemed to recognize his disturbance. Therefore, no one had considered that he needed help.

Mr. V. felt that his magical world had saved him from "going crazy." By that he meant his fantasy saved him from becoming enraged and attacking people. He remembered some instances of violent outbursts between himself and other foster children with whom he lived. The fights usually occurred after Mr. V. had been taunted and teased by the other children. He described his attacks on the other children as a mindless rushing and screaming at them like a "monster" with no thought of pain to himself. There were times when he had to be pulled away as he would not stop his hitting even if the child whom he was fighting was badly beaten.

SEXUALITY

During this period of his treatment, he was also able to explore how his current life situation and experiences were related to his childhood traumas. Without hesitation or embarrassment Mr. V. spoke about being "really turned on" by pornographic literature and films in which the theme was some form of sexual abuse and torture. Most exciting to him was viewing a woman using a mechanical torturing device on her male lover while at the same time having intercourse with him.

Mr. V. further revealed that he had frequented many prostitutes from the time he was 17, when he moved away from his final foster home placement and began to live on his own. Prostitutes were the only women who could "turn him on" as they would "do what I asked." He derived erotic satisfaction from intercourse if he was demeaned, threatened with torture, and physically made to feel helpless. For example, Mr. V. would ritualistically require the prostitute to tie or handcuff his arms and legs, after which she would berate him and threaten him with mutilation. He would seek out another prostitute whenever familiarity with one reduced the threat of danger.

Mr. V. thought that a major problem area at the beginning of his marriage had centered on his wife's disinterest in sexual intercourse almost immediately after the wedding. He had thought that he would be able to settle down and keep away from prostitutes. However, her sexual coldness was "unbearably painful" to him and exacerbated his need for prostitutes.

Also during that time, he had occasionally had sexual relations with male homosexual prostitutes who performed similar sexual rituals with him. During those encounters Mr. V. would come dangerously close to being arrested as they usually took place in public parks or other places where he could be easily seen and arrested. Mr. V. described his experience of excitement and sexual arousal at the thought of being publicly "despised." He had seen being tortured or demeaned as the "truthful" way that people related to him. It was therefore "relieving" not to expect otherwise and to live out the torture with prostitutes. He remembered thinking as a child that he would never trust anyone again, after his removal from his first foster home and the loss of his friend. When Mr. V.'s wife found out about his sexual activities, she left him and sought a divorce.

I understood Mr. V's ability to explore in detail his childhood traumatic experiences, and to relate those experiences to adult ones, as firm evidence of his growing trust in me as a comforting and understanding selfobject. For example, Mr. V. had never before revealed to anyone his need for intense sensation states at times of vulnerability and helplessness. Until now, he had felt that only the prostitutes could appreciate his needs, and that by fulfilling those needs they demonstrated an understanding of him.

We came to understand his longstanding requirements for intense stimulation as providing him with the needed self cohesion that had not been provided by age-appropriate transmuting internalization of the functions of reliable selfobjects. These intense feeling states can be viewed as a substitute for psychic structure.*

As Mr. V. continued the step-by-step exploration of the genetic determinants of his behavior, he came to realize the defensive importance of these powerful sensation states. We began to understand why he was not primarily concerned about the consequences of his behavior. The reason was that his need for intense stimulation took precedence over his need to preserve his personal and professional reputation. In the treatment he began to reconsider his behavior, which he had previously justified by rationalizing that people in general were corrupt and that his life-style was, therefore, what everyone else secretly wished theirs to be. Mr. V. went on to tell me that he had never really questioned his thinking about the corruptness of people before; it was something he had always taken for granted. He thought he

---

*It is well known that children who have structural deficiencies may perform a variety of physical actions such as head banging, rocking and spinning as well as frenetic activities. Whereas explanations vary according to one's theoretical persuasion, Kohut has suggested that such a child seeks stimulation in these actions in order to preserve and maintain cohesion of an enfeebled self (1971).

was able to question that now because his trust in me was leading him to "getting his hopes up" that the world might have something better to offer him.

WORKING THROUGH: MR. V.'S FANTASY LIFE

At this point in the treatment Mr. V. entered a working-through process which at times exacerbated his experience that I was depriving him. The heightened experience of being deprived came about as he began to (1) get in touch with his considerable potential, his talents, ambitions, and goals, and (2) move away from his sensation-producing sexual activities. While Mr. V.'s new hopefulness about the future led him to consider previously disavowed ambitions and goals and to move toward their implementation, it also threatened him with the loss of a life-style that had provided him with invaluable self-preservative stimulation.

He remembered how as a child he was fascinated with building and constructing a variety of structures with blocks and any other materials he could find. He remembered his interest in cutting out paper houses and creating a "village" of buildings, structures, people, animals, and the like from boxes and other cardboard products that he collected from his foster mother or found in his daily search of the trash baskets in his neighborhood. He cut all the figures to a certain scale and then carefully painted them.

Mr. V. was surprised that he remembered having any satisfaction as a child. As he spoke about those positive experiences, I got the impression that he became increasingly curious and motivated to understand what had happened to him in his development. He felt that it was like "waking up from a dream" to realize that there had been moments in his life that were worthwhile and times in his childhood when he had actually "looked forward to something." Mr. V. could not remember if anyone other than his foster mother's son had known how important creating his "village" was for him. For the most part he remembered playing with those structures alone and keeping them under his bed in a special place so that no one could see them.

There also were some vague memories of making some of his village structures in school and then taking them home to add to his collection. He recalled being very possessive of anything he made in school and not wanting to share it with classmates.

As Mr. V. got in touch with the importance of those creative times for him, he began to wonder how many of his creative interests must have been cut short by his life situation. He envisioned his involvement in designing and constructing his village as possibly leading to a number of professional interests if things had been different.

When he was removed from his first foster home placement, he no longer thought of constructing his figures. Rather, he began to focus on his forest world of friendly animals and vicious monsters. Mr. V. thought he had retreated then from trusting people and created a fantasy world of animals on whom he could rely.*

However, he felt strongly that even though he gave up the activity of constructing his "village," he never gave up his interest and curiosity in how and where people live. Now that he was becoming more aware of the importance of his interest in the

---

*Mr. V. thought of the animals in his imaginary forest as his "family." He was the only human member of this animal family. We eventually understood this fantasy as providing a form of comforting idealized selfobject figures. The monsters were representations of his pervasive expectation of being hurt and destroyed. His sometimes assuming the role of the monsters in play was his attempt at identifying with them through the defensive process of "identification with the aggressor" (A. Freud 1936). The eroticism he experienced was a consequence of the stimulation provided by the fantasized threat of destruction by the attacking monsters.

village's construction, he was able to recognize how that interest was evident even in his fantasy retreat to the forest of animals. Mr. V. pointed out that his imaginary conversations with his many animal friends had almost always focused on how and where they lived. He remembered not only the specific content of the imaginary dialogue but the special language that he and the animals spoke. During his sessions, Mr. V. demonstrated his elaborate way of making "animal" sounds that represented letters of the alphabet. In this way Mr. V. taught his imaginary animal friends to speak.

EMERGENCE OF A SECONDARY MIRROR TRANSFERENCE

As Mr. V. recaptured the experiences of his childhood deprivations and considered the effects these deprivations had had on the development of his nuclear talents and ambitions, he began to experience from a new perspective what had happened to him. For example, he was aware that his experience as a child was generally one of pervasive anxiety and expectation of danger. In addition, there had been times when his fear, anxiety, and confusion were so intense that he experienced lengthy periods of "numbness" and disorientation. Except for those instances when Mr. V. reacted violently against the children who taunted and teased him, he had been generally submissive.

He wondered why as a child he had not complained or at least told someone about his difficulties. Why had he been so compliant and subservient? As Mr. V. explored further his childhood experiences, we understood his compliance, his being the "good child," as a way of preventing any further unempathic reactions that might have resulted from his efforts at being independent. Conformity to the wishes of his foster parents also made it possible for Mr. V. to attain some modicum of caring and recognition, which he did not get when he was independently assertive.

As Mr. V. furthered his understanding of the meaning of his behavior, and the impact his childhood traumas had had on his adult life, he angrily resented the many circumstances and individuals that had contributed to his deprivation. During this time in the treatment, Mr. V. expressed his anger, further elaborated on the details of his traumatic experiences, and spontaneously shared with me what obviously was a highly creative way of thinking about making social changes in the adoption procedures. I was aware during this phase of the treatment that there was an emergence of a secondary mirror transference in which Mr. V. was trusting me to recognize and appreciate his increasingly insightful thinking, and especially his new vision and feeling about what had happened to him as a child. His incisive, logical, and to-the-point reasoning was in dramatic contrast to the generalized, vague, one-dimensional theme of "being ripped off" that had initially preoccupied him. Also, his anger was directed at more specific situations, such as the unempathic interchanges that had occurred with significant figures in his life. This, too, stood in dramatic contrast to the explosive reactive outbursts that had been characteristic of his earlier sessions.

As the secondary mirror selfobject transference developed, Mr. V. wished to intensify his treatment by increasing the number of sessions to three times a week. He specifically wished to do this because he was becoming "confused" as to what direction he should pursue as a major in his college studies, particularly since he found himself becoming disinterested in his managerial position.

Mr. V.'s Dreams

As Mr. V. increased the frequency of his treatment sessions in the beginning of the fourth year, he began to report and explore a number of dreams. Up until this point in the treatment, Mr. V. had remembered only parts of his dreams and showed little motivation to pursue his associations to uncover the meaning of those dream fragments that he did remember. I understood Mr. V.'s lack of motivation not so much as disinterest in his unconscious mental life but more as a consequence of his preoccupation with other priorities in the treatment. Mr. V. focused primarily on understanding the intensity of his potentially volatile reactions, and on their detrimental effects as they occurred with me in the treatment and with fellow students and business colleagues.

The urgency of his current situation therefore prevented in-depth dream analysis as well as associations to more detailed aspects of his traumatic childhood experiences. The third weekly session provided the needed treatment time to deepen his understanding and promote the transmuting internalization of the selfobject functions. As Mr. V.'s anxiety was reduced, the urgency of his current life situation was also reduced. Mr. V. was able to recall his dreams more in detail as his anxiety, which had interfered with his remembering, lessened.*

His dreams during the first month of his thrice-weekly treatment were predominantly what Kohut (1977) has described as "self-state dreams." As stated earlier, self-state dreams portray the dreamer's dread vis-à-vis some uncontrollable tension increase as a result of the dissolution of the self. The imagery

---

*Mr. V. sat up throughout his treatment. The use of the couch, which is one of the tools of psychoanalysis to promote regression, was considered inadvisable for Mr. V. in view of his pathology. Promoting regression might have further threatened him with the loss of self-cohesiveness.

portrayed in those dreams is an attempt to deal with the dangerous psychological nonverbal condition by organizing the traumatic states into verbalizable form. Unlike dreams in which the unconscious meanings of the underlying content (*latent* content) are uncovered through the patient's free associations, self-state dreams do not have hidden or underlying layers of meaning. Kohut thought that "self-state dreams" were similar to the dreams of children (Freud 1900), the dreams of those who have suffered traumatic neuroses (Freud 1920), and the hallucinatory dreams occurring with high fevers. These dreams are similar in that the meaning of the dream is contained in its obvious content (*manifest* content). Kohut also points out that a single dream may contain elements of self-state manifest content as well as of latent content (such as conflicts, wishes, confused solutions); it is the latter type that requires the patient's associations to uncover the unconscious meanings.

The first week that Mr. V. came for the increased number of sessions he reported a lengthy dream that embodied fragments of dreams that he was able to recall from earlier sessions. He described it as follows:

> It was nighttime. I was walking in a forest. It was similar to the forest I envisioned as a child when I had my imaginary animal friends. I kept walking but it was like I was not getting anywhere. It felt like the ground was moving backward as I went forward. Each step I took was in the same place as before. I kept walking but getting nowhere. Then the ground I was stepping on became some sort of cliff or precipice. I could not keep my balance. I felt paralyzed and unable to move and began to fall. I was waiting to die, but I didn't; I just kept falling, falling, and then I awoke.

Mr. V.'s associations led to his discovery of similar vague pervasive experiences of panic and helplessness as a child. He also

recalled specific feelings of helplessness, which he had not remembered before, at the time he was told that he would be placed
in his third foster home at the age of 11. He had been aware that
his second foster home placement was a temporary group foster
home. It was an emergency placement carried out when he was
around 7 years old after the discovery of the sexual abuse of his
first placement. However, when he received notice of his being
removed to a new foster home, he went through what he now
thought must have been some kind of a breakdown. He lost
interest in school and in general became more and more depressed. He specifically remembered his feelings of "heaviness"
and tiredness which reminded him now of the sensation in the
dream of not being able to move forward.

We understood this self-state dream as an attempt to depict
the overburdened condition of the self as he was coming to an
understanding of the extent of his deprivation, and of its consequences for him in his life. His association to his "breakdown"
gave us some understanding of what he was experiencing in the
present.

In brief, the dream imagery of walking can be understood as
symbolizing Mr. V.'s general movement ahead in the many
areas of his life (including his treatment) experience, and his
self-state experience of moving that finally culminated in helplessness, loss of control, and a terrifying fragmentation experience of falling endlessly. Important also was Mr. V.'s self-state
experience of his paralyzing expectations of dying while falling,
and his awareness that he did not die. Even though his anxiety
had awakened him, we understood his experience of surviving
his fall as evidence of a developing capacity to tolerate the nearly
overwhelming anxiety precipitated by his new awareness and
his pursuit of previously thwarted goals.

Mr. V. was both upset and relieved by his understanding of
his dream. On the one hand he was concerned that his previous

reliance on his imaginary forest and animal friends was no longer providing the same soothing function it had had. On the other hand, Mr. V. was relieved that in the dream he was able to withstand the nearly intolerable feelings of helplessness before awakening. He thought that his coming more often would help him get in touch with the intensity of his fears, because he felt that I would understand the depth of his pain and feelings of helplessness. However, it was hard for him to believe that he could continue to rely on me "to be there for him." Maybe someday I would get rid of him, like everybody else did.

In the following months Mr. V. reported a number of self-state dreams with similar themes of falling and destruction. Some of the dreams contained imagery of the forest of his childhood. For example, in one self-state dream,

> Mr. V. was climbing a stairway that was at one end of a long hallway. He climbed to the top of the stairway which led to the ceiling of the hallway. As he attempted to walk back down, the stairs began to topple. Mr. V. began to fall helplessly. The stairs disappeared and Mr. V. fell faster and faster past tree-tops and somehow landed face down on a tree limb that was high above the ground. He was frozen with fear. He could not maintain his balance. Slowly, he felt his outstretched body slipping off the side of the limb. He was helpless to keep his balance and began to fall again, but this time with his back to the ground. He was unable to turn himself over in order to get some control over the fall and to see where he was falling. Still unable to move or exert control over his body, Mr. V. began to float downward and forward "like a glider" until he came to a smooth and relaxed landing on his back. His anxiety returned, however, as he struggled to raise himself. He awoke in an anxious state while trying to sit.

A major difference in this self- state dream from the previous one was Mr. V.'s experience of floating to an easy and relaxed landing. He described the experience of floating downward while lying on his back as being frightening but at the same time soothing and relieving. His associations led him to remembering the details of a childhood game that he had played with his friend in his first foster placement. In this game, he would fall backward and trust that his friend would catch him. The object of the game was to see how close to the floor he could allow himself to fall while trusting his friend to catch him. The two boys played this game daily and Mr. V. soon trusted his friend to catch him at the level of the floor.

Mr. V. associated his feeling of floating in the dream to the calm he experienced at times when he meditated. He was relieved, as in his initial self-state dream, that he was able to tolerate the paralyzing fear and was even able to experience some comfort despite what he described as "an anxiety which reached nightmarish intensity."

Unlike with his initial dream, Mr. V. did not offer any associations to his developing trust in me (idealizing selfobject transference) as contributing to his capacity to tolerate the intensity of his anxiety. Nor did Mr. V. associate to his developing reliance on me as contributing to the comforting experience of floating in the dream. I understood, however, that even though Mr. V.'s associations to the comforting aspects of the dream led only to the trusting experiences with his childhood friend, it can be assumed that the dream also embodied the soothing experience Mr. V. was allowing to develop with me. It can be suggested that he would not have been able to recover the trusting experiences with his friend unless some structure-building processes had taken place through the transmuting internalization of my anxiety-relieving functions as an empathic selfobject.

However, it can also be postulated that Mr. V.'s becoming anxious again at the end of the dream, when he attempted to get up after the smooth and comforting landing, was an indication that (1) there was not sufficient internalization of these soothing selfobject functions in the idealizing sector; and (2) there was insufficient working through of Mr. V.'s anxiety in moving toward his goals.

In general I understood that Mr. V.'s anxiety-relieving experience in the dream, of floating, moving forward, and landing smoothly, represented a moving away from his fantasy forest for comfort.

Within the context of the predominant secondary mirror transference, I was aware that Mr. V.'s idealizing needs were again slowly unfolding as he moved from experiencing my understanding the depth of his deprivation as a child to my now understanding his newly evolving goals and ambitions as an adult.

His Emerging Ambitions and Goals

A pivotal time in Mr. V.'s treatment was his deciding on a major in his course of study to complete his bachelor's degree. He had taken a wide range of courses that interested him and could be credited toward four possible major courses of study. These were psychology, sociology, business, and physics. He also, for a short time, considered becoming an architect, which was in keeping with his boyhood interest in the construction and design of his "village." However, he realized that as he was becoming more interested and involved in understanding himself, he was at the same time becoming motivated and curious to understand others. He was aware of his shift in treatment from viewing the "system" as "ripping him off" to experiencing concern for others who were as disadvantaged as he had been as a child.

Mr. V. decided on sociology as his college major. He thought that the study of social phenomena would bring together his interests in how social systems work and their effects on the individual. Much of his focus during this time and until termination was on elaborating, exploring, and refining his ideas about social and political issues. Whereas he freely shared with me his evolving ideas of social change, he did so with the continuous expectation that I would at some point misunderstand him and oppose him in some manner that would "take everything away." He explained that he could envision the possibility of my suddenly becoming disdainful of his ideas. He would then realize that his becoming hopeful that people would care to understand him, and that there could be a better society, was only another trick of his mind.

I understood that Mr. V.'s expectation of a traumatic "wipe-out" of his hopefulness was reemerging now as a result of his pursuing his ambitions and goals. The reemergence of the fears and anxieties associated with genetically analogous situations is expectable as part of the working-through process. As any patient moves closer toward the fulfillment of previously thwarted needs and the implementation of his or her constitutional endowment and nuclear design, the patient will experience the revival of those childhood traumas that are associated with the thwarted needs. A successful working through of the interfering, telescoped, genetically analogous traumatic situation continues until the nuclear defects have been exposed and there has been a development of reliable compensatory structure (Kohut 1977). The working through takes place as the treatment deepens through the interpretative (explaining) process, in terms of what happened to him as a child (genetic), the intensity of his experiences (economic), and the effect of these experiences on his intrapsychic development (dynamic).

As Mr. V. continued to share his many ideas about social change, and worked through the telescoped fears of my rejecting him, I was aware that in the development of his thoughts he was moving away from the more global, universal, and less sophisticated ideas and plans to more specific, detailed, and carefully thought-out ones.

The development of his thinking took place as he was simultaneously able to explore and work through his initial powerful grandiose desires for making sweeping social changes through punitive legislation. Much of the working-through process was precipitated by his experiencing the rejection of his ideas by a number of his classmates, and especially by one instructor who threatened to drop him from a course as Mr. V. was upsetting other students with his radical ideas and his tendency to interrupt and monopolize class discussions. He described a range of experiences at these times of criticism from feeling "confused" to feeling "subdued," and at times "devastated." However, he was able to tolerate these difficult experiences without reacting defensively. He was able to listen to the criticism and discuss the effects of his behavior. He was also able to comply with his instructor's demand to limit his comments.

Mr. V.'s Search for All-Accepting Selfobjects

During this time Mr. V. experienced a period of intense depression and fleeting thoughts of suicide. He shared with me his sense of hopelessness that he would ever be understood or accepted by his colleagues. Why should he continue his studies? His worst fears in regard to trusting others to understand him were coming true. The rug was being pulled out from under him once again.

Mr. V.'s new ability to listen to his instructor's and classmates' criticism indicated that he had accrued substantial self structure to withstand the potentially fragmenting experience of being criticized. His depression and feelings of hopelessness, while severe, indicated that he was able to tolerate telescoped experiences of despair, as well as to tolerate his awareness of the spectrum of relentless traumas which had occurred over time – an experiential overview which would previously have been intolerable to Mr. V., who had struggled day by day to survive.

As Mr. V. worked through his feelings of hopelessness and despair, he came to the awareness (1) that he expected everyone to understand him, no matter how radical his ideas, and (2) that his expectation for in-depth analytic understanding was appropriate within the treatment but not outside it with friends and colleagues. This latter awareness was initially upsetting in that it meant that he had to be aware of the needs and limitations of others. Now that he was finally able to feel free to share his thinking in treatment without constrictions, he wished to do so outside of treatment.

He spoke of his disillusionment with me and the treatment as not providing him with an "ideal world," like his childhood fantasy forest world of friendly animals. As we explored his disappointment in me and the treatment, we understood that his hopes for the ideal world that treatment failed to provide was understandable within the context of his severe and pervasive deprivations, which had left him searching for an all-understanding parental figure. Kohut (1971) taught that the longing and searching for the perfect idealized selfobject comes about as a consequence of fixations on archaic forms of parental images due to early and traumatic disillusionments.

Mr. V. was able to explore and analyze further his unrequited longing and his disappointment in me. Little by little he began to reveal that he was listening to and considering the views of his classmates and instructors in regard to his presentations, and was being recognized and complimented by them for his attention to their ideas. He experienced the compliments from his instructor as "nice," but he still longed for the intensity of his previously uninhibited expressions and wished for the unconditional acceptance of his ideas.

Slowly he was developing a growing capacity to listen and be attuned to the needs of his classmates, even though this attunement deprived him of his primitive grandiosity. I attributed the development of his accruing self-soothing structure to the continuing transmuting internalization of the empathic functions that I provided him with through the treatment. His disillusionment, which he was able to tolerate, facilitated the transmuting internalization process (Kohut 1971).

In time, Mr. V.'s generalized experience of being deprived of unrestricted expression and unqualified recognition subsided. Concomitantly, he experienced more satisfaction when his instructors and colleagues showed interest in him. For example, he no longer thought their attention was just "nice"; rather he felt proud when he was recognized as making constructive points. He frequently volunteered to make presentations in class and organized a study group to study a variety of community problems.

During this time Mr. V. began to date and ultimately have an affair with a young woman who was one of his classmates. He described her as unlike his wife in important ways. Whereas his wife had had a great interest in material wealth and pushed Mr. V. to make more and more money, his current friend appreciated Mr. V. for the way he thought about things and especially his views on social change. He continued to see this young woman throughout his three remaining years of part-time undergraduate study.

Also during this time, Mr. V.'s need for the highly charged erotic sensations that he had sought with prostitutes diminished considerably. Similar to what we touched upon in the earlier discussion of Ms. O.'s case, his sexual experience with his woman friend was initially described by him as "too tame and caring" in comparison to the intense erotic sensations he had achieved by dangerously engaging in illegal sexual activity.

As Mr. V. explored the quality of his previous highly erotic sexual sensations and that of his current experience, he was concerned that he was depriving himself of what he called "real sex." At times he suggested to his woman friend that they engage in various sexual games that involved other people, costumes, and a variety of sexual devices. She refused to consider these ideas and suggested that he find someone else if such activities were important to him. He did not want to insist because he was certain that she would leave him as his wife had when she found out about his sexual exploits.

Mr. V. explored in further detail his sexual experience with his wife who, in contrast to his current friend, had rarely initiated affectionate contact. He remembered his continuous feeling of being physically ignored that had started almost immediately after the marriage. As he repeatedly indicated, he had longed for intense sexual sensation to make him feel alive. It was different now, however, in that he did not think he needed the intensity as before, even though he desired a heightened eroticism. By this, Mr. V. thought that now he was primarily seeking the heightened erotic sensations for the pleasure they would provide for his firmer and more stable self, and not so much for relief of the pervasive intolerable feeling of emptiness and vulnerability he had experienced earlier in treatment. He described himself as "addicted" to intense erotic sensations. However, he was aware that his desire for heightened sensation states was preventing him from fully appreciating the closeness with his current woman friend who he knew cared very much for him.

As was discussed earlier, it can be pointed out here that patients who have been severely traumatized frequently seek intense erotic sensations even after sufficient self structure has accrued, and when there is no longer a need for intense sensations as a substitute for the missing self structure. For example, Mr. V.'s continuing craving for heightened erotic sensations and the pervasiveness and strength of his compulsion for intense sexual encounters suggested a dependency on the intensity that these erotic feeling states provided. The achievement of intense erotic feeling states became for him the focus of sexual relations and the criterion of sexual compatibility. Patients who have suffered similar traumas frequently describe tender, less intense responses by their partners as "boring" or as evidence of sexual incompatibility. This is usually true even with a patient who acknowledges his or her partner's tenderness as an expression of caring, as was the case with Mr. V.

Equating eroticism with love or with sexual compatibility is understandable not only as a result of the patient's dependency on intense sensations, but also as a consequence of the patient's having been deprived of prototypical experiences with caring selfobjects. That is, these traumatized patients have not been afforded the opportunity to have ongoing, consistently caring selfobject experiences throughout their development, which eventually become the fundamental constituents of healthy adult sexuality.

However, as compensatory structures develop and as selfobject needs unfold, patients are introduced to new experiences of closeness that can replace the equation of eroticism and love, and lessen the dependency on intense sensation states. For example, Mr. V. was aware that his friend cared for him very much and that he did not want to risk alienating her by continuing to suggest erotic depersonalized sexual activities. Mr. V.'s friendship had become more important and meaningful to him than his desire for erotic sensations. He abstained from erotic sexual practices in order to preserve his friendship. His dependency on intense sensations subsided as he became more and more receptive and appreciative of her affection for him. His appreciation of her kindness developed as he realized that his reference for evaluating successful sexual relations with women was based on the degree of erotic intensity that he achieved through depersonalized sexual activities. Mr. V. was surprised that he actually began to enjoy what he described as "being human." By this he meant that he could feel loving and sexual feelings simultaneously.

In sum, Mr. V.'s appreciation of his friend grew over the next months. He wished to become engaged. After thorough analysis of this wish, we understood his desire to marry and build a life with her as a continuation of his development, whereby he could have an admiring and supportive helpmate (selfobject) toward whom he could also be admiring and helpful.

Mr. V. became engaged and he and his fiancée were married soon after they graduated. He contiued to work in his managerial position after graduation, and decided to continue his part-time studies toward a doctorate in sociology with the goal of eventually working in the public sector. His wife, who had earned a degree in education, also began part-time graduate studies while working as a teacher.

TERMINATION

Termination of treatment was planned approximately a year after he entered graduate school. We were in accord that he had achieved substantial developmental gains. During the period of termination, Mr. V. expressed his gratitude about our years of work and a quiet confidence in his ability to pursue his goals. While he was sad that we were ending our work, his hopefulness about the future and his feelings of confidence helped to make termination a mutually positive experience.

Mr. V.'s analysis was in keeping with what Kohut considered a successful treatment (see Chapter 7). For example, Mr. V. had developed compensatory structure in the idealizing sector of the self as evidenced by the developmental unfolding of his idealizing needs, first in the treatment and then with his wife. Mr. V.'s pursuant sophisticated idealized goals via his studies in sociology is further evidence of the development of compensatory structure in the idealizing pole of the self.

He had also developed compensatory structure in the exhibitionistic (grandiose) sector as evidenced by his pursuing and implementing his scholastic goals and his plans to effect change in the social system. His marriage, and his ongoing efforts to strengthen and preserve the marriage through planning for mutual educational growth, are further evidence of realization of development of the grandiose self.

Implicit in his development was Mr. V.'s awareness of the deficits in his self structure and how those deficits came about as a consequence of a deeply depriving early selfobject milieu. Mr. V. came to understand how his deprivations had led him to need erotic stimulation to revitalize an enfeebled self, and had established a prototype of sexual experience that he equated with affection and love. A final factor significant in a successful analysis is the patient's finding and establishing a wider circle of satisfying selfobjects. Mr. V.'s rewarding associations with classmates and instructors further indicated the success of the treatment.

In his final session there were expressions of loss, although the overall tone was one of gratitude for what had been achieved and excitement with the prospects of what lay ahead. He departed with a warm and firm handshake, laughingly adding that "maybe I'll bump into you sometime." The only contact after the treatment was a note from him some two years later indicating that he had received his master's degree.

CHAPTER 19

The

Empathic–Introspective

Approach

In the preceding chapters, we have presented Heinz Kohut's essential contributions. It is our hope that the issues raised in this book have been helpful not only to the seasoned psychoanalyst, but also to the student of psychoanalysis and psychotherapy, as well as to those interested readers outside the mental health field.

Throughout our summary, we have stressed the empathic–introspective approach. From this experience-near vantage point, Kohut gathered his data and developed his theories in a manner similar to that of Freud in his formulations of earlier theories. The important point here is that Kohut systematized the experience-near empathic vantage point as the basic structure upon which the treatment process is built. In other words, there can be no treatment (understanding and explaining) without adhering to and employing this empathic stance.

Kohut emphasized throughout his writings that this approach offers us an avenue of research through which we can continue to deepen and widen our theoretical understanding of complex mental states.

To oversimplify for a moment, we learn, organize our theories, and direct our explanations to what the patient is experiencing. We do not attempt to persuade, direct, or impose no matter how convinced we are of our own understandings. The analyst keeps in mind that interventions are at best approximations of the truth, and subject to continuous correction by the patient. In this way there is a mutual learning process, not one in which the analyst attempts to get the patient to accept an interpretation through some form of negotiation of different positions, in an effort to arrive at a meeting of the minds (Goldberg 1987).

Kohut has also made it clear throughout his writings that the treatment process is one in which the needs of the patient are understood and interpreted in dynamic, genetic, and economic terms. In other words, empathy is used not for gratification but rather for understanding and explaining. The mirroring and idealizing needs are understood and analyzed, not actively gratified through some verbal or nonverbal evaluative "pat on the back."

For example, as we discussed in the case of Mr. V.'s purchase of a newly tailor-made jacket and pants, the emphasis was on understanding the fullness of his experience of enthusiasm and the wish for admiration of his choice. It would have been an active gratification, and therefore an error in the treatment, if the analyst had in some way approved of or complimented Mr. V. on his choice. Of course, we recognize that the patient's feeling understood is also a form of gratification. However, whereas feeling understood facilitates the treatment, active gratification by means of compliments and so on interferes with the understanding process and therefore the treatment. This is well documented in the analytic literature.

This new frontier of understanding has brought about a reconsideration of what comprises analytic treatment. Traditionally, treatment could be defined as psychoanalysis if the patient substantially revived heretofore repressed infantile conflicts which had been brought forward through levels of psychosexual development, and expressed within the oedipal configuration as a transference neurosis. The patient is usually seen on the couch at a minimum of four times per week.

We would suggest that, within the framework of self psychology, psychoanalysis can be defined as that treatment process that allows for the development of the selfobject transferences, and makes possible the uncovering of the patient's nuclear defects and the eventual development of compensatory structure through the working-through process.

Within this definition Ms. O. and Mr. V. can be considered to have undergone successful analysis even though the frequency of their treatment sessions was less than the traditional four times per week. In addition, Ms. O. utilized the couch whereas Mr. V. sat throughout the treatment. This suggests that certain of the usual criteria for defining what is psychoanalysis, such as the frequency of sessions and the use of the couch, must be reexamined within the new understanding of complex mental states offered by self psychology.

Self psychology has also offered additional understanding of the function of fantasy in meeting selfobject needs. For example,

Mr. V.'s childhood fantasy of the "forest world" provided him with a soothing and idealizing experience, as well as a twinship fantasy experience with his imaginary community of animal friends.* This understanding of Mr. V.'s fantasy contrasts with the traditional view of fantasy as a compromise formation that expresses and gratifies unconscious instinctual wishes.

We have not only presented examples that highlight the clinical application of the theory of self psychology in a general way, but we have also attempted to give the reader a detailed moment-to-moment view of treatment as illustrated by the cases of Ms. O. and Mr. V. This method of presentation made it possible to illustrate our concept of "expanding attunement," which alerts the analyst to the unfolding of the nuances of a patient's shifting selfobject needs as well as to the resistances against their unfolding. We have attempted through our experience-near method of presentation to reflect the very message that self psychology is trying to teach.

It is important to note that, even though Ms. O. and Mr. V. had suffered severe traumatic deprivations that resulted in fixations in the idealizing sectors of the self, they were able to recover repressed positive idealizing experiences, albeit limited and not consistent with any one selfobject of childhood. Even so, they were able to recover those limited and positive selfobject experiences and build upon them in the treatment. This suggests that the self psychological treatment approach offers a prognostically hopeful outcome for even the most disturbed among our patient population. Perhaps it is just this hopefulness that is one of Kohut's most valuable and lasting contributions.

---

*Compare Mr. V's idealizing fantasy experience with Kohut's patient who had a sustaining twinship fantasy with her "genie in the bottle" described earlier.

References

Atwood, G., and Stolorow, R. (1984). *Structures of Subjectivity: Explorations in Psychoanalytic Phenomenology*. Hillsdale, New Jersey: The Analytic Press.

Basch, M. F. (1980). *Doing Psychotherapy*. New York: Basic Books, Inc.

Beebe, B., and Sloate, P. (1982). Assessment and treatment of difficulties in mother-infant attunement in the first three years of life: a case history. *Psychoanalytic Inquiry* 1:601-623.

Elkisch, P. (1957). The psychological significance of the mirror. *Journal of the American Psychoanalytic Association* 5:235-244.

Freud, A. (1936). *The Ego and Mechanics of Defense. The Writings of Anna Freud.* Vol. 2. Rev. ed. New York: International Universities Press.

Freud, S. (1900). The interpretation of dreams. *Standard Edition* 4/5: 1–361.

——— (1912). Recommendations to physicians practising psychoanalysis. *Standard Edition* 12:111–120.

——— (1915). Instincts and their vicissitudes. *Standard Edition* 14:117–140.

——— (1920). Beyond the pleasure principle. *Standard Edition* 18:7–64.

Goldberg, A., ed. (1978). *The Psychology of the Self: A Casebook.* New York: International Universities Press.

——— (1982). Obituary: Heinz Kohut. *International Journal of Psycho-Analysis* 63:257–258.

——— (1987). Psychoanalysis and negotiation. *The Psychoanalytic Quarterly* 56:109–129.

——— (1988). *A Fresh Look at Psychoanalysis: The View from Self Psychology.* Hillsdale, N.J.: The Analytic Press.

Hartmann, H. (1950). Comments on the psychoanalytic theory of the ego. In *Essays on Ego Psychology: Selected Problems in Psychoanalytic Theory,* pp. 113–141. New York: International Universities Press.

Kernberg, O. (1968). The treatment of patients with borderline personality organization. *International Journal of Psycho-Analysis* 49:600–619.

——— (1971). Prognostic considerations regarding borderline personality organization. *Journal of the American Psychoanalytic Association* 19:595–635.

——— (1975). *Borderline Conditions and Pathological Narcissism.* New York: Jason Aronson.

Knight, R. P. (1953). Borderline states. In *Drives, Affects, Behavior,* ed. R.M. Lowenstein, pp. 203–215. New York: International Universities Press.

Kohut, H. (1951). Discussion of Samuel D. Lipton's paper: the function of the analyst in the therapeutic process. In *The Search for the Self,* vol. 1, ed. P.H. Ornstein, pp. 159–166. New York: International Universities Press.

_____ (1959). Introspection, empathy, and psychoanalysis: an examination of the relationship between mode of observation and theory. In *The Search for the Self*, vol. 1, ed. P.H. Ornstein, pp. 205-232. New York: International Universities Press.

_____ (1966). Forms and transformations of narcissism. *Journal of the American Psychoanalytic Association* 14:243-272.

_____ (1968). The psychoanalytic treatment of narcissistic personality disorders, outline of a systematic approach. *The Psychoanalytic Study of the Child* 23:86-113.

_____ (1971). *The Analysis of the Self*. New York: International Universities Press.

_____ (1974). Letter of May 16, 1974. In *The Search for the Self*, vol. 2, ed. P.H. Ornstein, pp. 888-891. New York: International Universities Press.

_____ (1975a). Remarks about the formation of the self. In *The Search for the Self*, vol. 2, ed. P.H. Ornstein, pp. 737-770. New York: International Universities Press.

_____ (1975b). A note on female sexuality. In *The Search for the Self*, vol. 2, ed. P.H. Ornstein, pp. 783-792. New York: International Universities Press.

_____ (1977). *The Restoration of the Self*. New York: International Universities Press.

_____ (1979). The two analyses of Mr. Z. *International Journal of Psycho-Analysis* 60:3-27.

_____ (1984). *How Does Analysis Cure?* Chicago: The University of Chicago Press.

Kohut, H., and Wolf, E. (1978). The disorders of the self and their treatment: an outline. *International Journal of Psycho-Analysis* 59:413-425.

Leo, J., (1980, December). The preacher of narcissism. *Time Magazine*, p. 76.

Lichtenstein, H. (1961). Identity and sexuality: a study of their interrelationship in man. *Journal of the American Psychoanalytic Association* 9:179-260.

_____ (1964). The role of narcissism in the emergence and maintenance of a primary identity. *International Journal of Psycho-Analysis* 45:49–56.

Mahler, M. (1968). *On Human Symbiosis and the Vicissitudes of Individuation.* New York: International Universities Press.

Meltzoff, A., and Moore, M. (1977). Initiation of facial and manual gestures by human neonates. *Science* 198:75–78.

Montgomery, P. (1981, October 10). Obituary – Heinz Kohut. *The New York Times*, p. 17.

Ornstein, P. H. (1978). Introduction: The evolution of Heinz Kohut's psychoanalytic psychology of the self. In *The Search for the Self*, vol. 1, ed. P.H. Ornstein, pp. 1–106. New York: International Universities Press.

Sander, L.W. (1962). Issues in early mother–child interaction. *Journal of the American Academy of Child Psychiatry* 1:141–166.

_____ (1964). Adaptive relationships in early mother–child interaction. *Journal of the American Academy of Child Psychiatry* 3:231–264.

Schwaber, E. (1979). On the "self" within the matrix of analytic theory. Some clinical reflections and reconsiderations. *International Journal of Psycho-Analysis* 60:467–479.

Stechler, G. (1982). The dawn of awareness. *Psychoanalytic Inquiry* 1:503–532.

Stern, D. N. (1983). The early development of schemas of self, other, and "self with other." In *Reflections on Self Psychology*, ed. J. Lichtenberg and S. Kaplan, pp. 49–84. Hillsdale, N.J.: The Analytic Press.

Stolorow, R., Brandchaft, B., and Atwood, G. (1987). *Psychoanalytic Treatment, an Intersubjective Approach.* Hillsdale, N.J.: The Analytic Press.

Strozier, C. B. (1985). Glimpses of a life: Heinz Kohut (1913–81). In *Progress in Self Psychology*, vol. 1, ed. A. Goldberg, pp. 3–12. New York: The Guilford Press.

Wolf, E. S. (1976). Ambience and abstinence. *Annual of Psychoanalysis* 4:101–115.

_____ (1988). *Treating the Self: Elements of Clinical Self Psychology.* New York: The Guilford Press.

Index

About the Authors

Crayton E. Rowe, Jr., received an M.S.W. from Hunter College School of Social Work. He is a member and Training Analyst for The New York Freudian Society and the National Psychological Association for Psychoanalysis. He is a founding member of the New York Institute for Psychoanalytic Self Psychology, chairman of the national membership committee on psychoanalysis of the National Federation of Societies for Clinical Social Work, and was elected a Distinguished Practitioner of Social Work of the National Academies of Practice. Rowe is a clinical supervisor at the University Settlement Consultation Center and maintains a private practice in psychoanalysis and psychotherapy in New York City.

David S. Mac Isaac, Ph.D., received his training at Fordham University and the New York Center for Psychoanalytic Training. He is a section one member of the Division of Psychoanalysis of the American Psychological Association. Dr. Mac Isaac is a board member of the Institute for Psychoanalysis and Psychotherapy of New Jersey and a founding member of the New York Institute for Psychoanalytic Self Psychology. He maintains a private practice in psychotherapy and psychoanalysis in Englewood, New Jersey.

Made in the USA
San Bernardino, CA
19 August 2013